The Phoenix with the Chrystal Plumage

"The Immortality"

VIE Loriot de Rouvray

The Phoenix With The Chrystal Plumage
"The Immortality"
Copyright © 2024 by VIE Loriot de Rouvray
All rights reserved.

ISBN: 979-8-9905885-0-9 Paperback
ISBN: 979-8-9905885-1-6 Hardback

One Life Many Solutions,
Une Vie Plusieurs Solutions,
Una Vida Mas Soluciones

"It is Time to Soar into the Cosmic Wonders"
The Phoenix with the Crystal Plumage is a living
Spirit Protector of Writers

Note for the Readers

In my work as an author, a spiritual counselor teacher, and a visionary intuitive healer on a mission to re-connect people, this book brings you a fresh perspective to ancient wisdom and is important in the field, and the topic of spiritual development. It is important for the opening of the consciousness and your transformation.

As two angels sent to work on earth the Spirit of GOD guided us on this new Journey, and what a journey of Discovery. The first thing they did when they found us was to cut CHADD's wings and assault his and my physical body.

Welcome to an adventure when the curtains are about to open. At that time Saint Michael the Archangel appeared physically to me. This is it. There is no turning back. The events of our time are deeply upsetting. We are about to ascend. This is a fascinating adventure that has taken all my time.

For most people, let's say that there are two realities. Yours, that is a holographic reality that keeps you in a loop from which you seem not to be able to break, and mine. You have been trapped by lies in TV fake news from the well-paid media that and through your TV screen that hypnotized you and made you believe in the false reality. But you need to be able to awaken to ascend. My writings are stories and words encoded to help you. This is one part of CHADD's ghostwriting and my mission. The highest Government of the Universe has sent us to help you. But be aware that I work directly under God. You must acknowledge him if you want to make it. Jesus will come back whether you want or not and you better know him. The era of darkness is finished. The era of the controller and the worshiper of money is gone. Love conquers all, and the Light will touch the darkest depths of each and everyone's soul. You must let the light approach and enter inside your soul.

Real white magic does not require candles, uniforms, and power objects. Real white magic is of the same irradiation as the disciple who is aligned with the divine purpose, who, wherever he passes, is transmuting the environment around him. Even the Universe goes down on its knees and aliens itself to this Devine Plan of which the Conscious Being is an active part.

In this new age of enlightenment, pursuing knowledge and wisdom will take priority over material gain. The thirst for understanding will drive you to explore the farthest reaches of the cosmos, unlocking the secrets of distant galaxies and ancient civilizations.

As all take this quantum leap in evolution, remember that you are not alone in this journey. Together, let us rise and shine, illuminating the cosmos with the brilliance of awakened souls. Journeying through the corridors of time and space, the mysteries of the universe shall be revealed, and the secrets of existence will be laid bare before all.

Prepare for the dawn of a new age. A celestial fabric of possibilities awaits, woven with the threads of imagination and realized through the harmonious union of science and spirit.

Preface

In writing this new book, I am conscious that my purpose, our mission, and our work as the God Duo might be criticized by unfaithful or unweakened beings. And it's OK. I am sure that they will still give them some reflection to help them be opened, and awakened, helped them grow.

I am aware that it will take time to accept and internally receive. It will take some time to believe, as the long journey to earth has erased most of the memory, the knowing, the feeling when it is right in front of you but eventually, this will be you're in the natural state of being.

"This is part of a New Thrilling Adventure, of a series of books. A Journey to the Unknown and a Quest to Self-Mastery with an Angelic Couple on an Earth Mission. They are called to teach and to guide you, they are named CHADD & VIE. Known as the God Duo, sent by the highest Government of the Universe."

The story begins with Henri the granddaddy married to Martha, and their son Edward who was contacted by the NSA to work for the government. Edward married Ethel and they had a son, CHADD. Edward divorced later and remarried Katherine.

At age five the government started to do testing on CHADD to understand his abilities. They found out that his DNA had been altered. CHADD was given multiple psychotropic drugs. He fell into a few months' coma after an overdose of prescription drugs and became blind, anemic, and incontinent due to the pharmaceutical drugs. He was placed in various state hospitals and became in custody of the state.

VIE found out that Katherine, CHADD's father's second wife, was an archon and reptilian bloodline when one day she saw her shapeshifting.

During CHADD's stay at the hospital, a group called the Guardians revealed themselves. They have existed throughout history. They were the Cathari. There were two groups: The Perfecti and the Believers. The Perfecti helped defeat Hitler and the Believers were the Nazis.

They are serial killers and now want revenge against humanity. Extremely intelligent and hypnotizing at the same time, some of the Believers had guidance in genetic reproduction thousands of years ago, before and after the great flood, to create creatures seen as vampires, bigfoot, and reptilians. The Cathari were the descendants of the angels in the book of Enoch that mated with earthly women.

The Perfecti took the virtues of love and kindness, and the Believers in the love of money, power, pain, and destruction. The Indian Thuggees re-materialized infiltrated and took control of state hospitals.

This time while CHADD is kept under the care of the harsh woman, Katherine, who works for the elite in power, he is forced to continue to ingest psychotropic drugs ordered by the court and prescribed by a psychiatrist doctor they designated. And now VIE is viciously attacked.

VIE is attacked by the black mentalists and then by Katherine after visiting a thirteen-century Gothic Cathedral in France where VIE was guided to go. In the Gothic Cathedral VIE used her Vajra, spoke the language of the Light, and anchored and activated some new frequencies.

The words of the language of the Light contain vibrational frequencies to upgrade your energetic field to make the shift, and the integration through this process is much easier for you to maneuver.

When one-day VIE's life changed drastically after the reunion with her blue flame, she entered a world of conspiracy and lies. She is told that they are two angels at work sent by the highest government in the world on a Galactic mission. VIE is the door to the Divine. CHADD is a baker act drugged UP ward of the state, kept on drugs, and holds the keys to the Divine wisdom. He is sent from one mental hospital to another by the corrupted justice system, and the drugs disable his brain's ability to filter information, blocking signals to his consciousness.

VIE as a metaphysical light & vibratory healer works with vibrational transformation energy. She is bringing knowledge and the hidden truth to the masses of people. It is the time when the elite will be overthrown. The elite are the dynasties, the families of wealth and privilege, and those in control since the dawn of civilization who worship Lucifer.

They are the God Duo, and they came back to guide and inform you with some important information, and to bring you oneness. It is the time of awakening and remembering because people have been misguided by the institutions, religions, and churches and it is sad. But the world is living the last final battle between God and the governments, a world prison system by the government.

It's a system where law and money are integrated to bind the world population by and in that system. It's a world prison created to train that population to willingly consent to voluntarily bind themselves—to be essentially bonded servants to that system to become the mechanism by which the resources, the wealth of the world which comes from, all the natural resources, to be the mechanism to harvest, that reach the resources, to build out the global civilization that we live in today.

It is a modern adventure lived by the God Duo with tribulations through which Christianity is introduced to the world and demonstrates the path to Divine love.

The black mentalists are the same evil forces that destroyed Atlantis. When they found out that VIE was in the medieval city. They felt threatened. They made it all impossible for her to meet with one of the knights Templars she was supposed to. One designated black mentalist kept materializing and dematerializing following her on her trip to the medieval city.

A man with a bag-pack and a woman were waiting for her inside the Gothic Cathedral and felt threatened by her, so poisoned her food twice. This was before the spiritual attack on the back of her neck with a big black wound, then the attack on the right side of the neck lymph. Then she was awakened in the middle of the night with horrible pain. They nailed the middle of her palms, her wrists, and every phalanges on both hands. VIE did not realize immediately what was happening to her, and when she called for protection from Saint Michael the Archangel it was too late.

The Cathari is the link to the Catholic. The Cathari is all hidden power and becomes the Knight Templar forgotten by the Catholics. There are two elements to Cathari. The Perfecti and the Believers. The perfecti are the ones that want to bring people to God. They helped defeat Hitler, protected women and children, and then disappeared into another time. While the Believers were the Nazis. The Gothic Cathedral in Carcassonne is dedicated to Archangel Michael and connected to the lineage of Mary Magdalene.

The content of this book acts as a bridge between the mystical realms in the path of humans' awakening. As we can see, the world is dramatically changing, and the spiritual path is changing with it. Not only it will be a new world but also a new spiritual path that will be inclusive of your multidimensional energetic self fully integrated into the path of awakening that is rooted and based in the heart. With the focus being to remember the light that you are and the return to the love you have always been.

The Gregorian Calendar and the Gregorian chant were created by Saint Gregory, Gregory the Great, and Gregory is still of the existing Templar. Knight Templars are back on Earth. Albassinian is connected to Avignon and the Knight Templar. "Les Cercles blancs" which are two circles that interconnect Albasinnian (that means white)

Now listen carefully, RA was the Ancient Builder Race. "The purpose of incarnate existence is the evolution of mind, body, and spirit" Ra, Law of one."

Out there in the universe, humans are very dangerous. Violent, unpredictable, and uncontrollable. Some aliens/extraterrestrials have been monitoring the Earth for some time. They are part of the Kuiper Belt group (also known as the Edgeworth–Kuiper belt) it is a region of the Solar System that exists beyond the eight major planets and has an agenda to remove the Deep State from this planet.

The Deep State and the hybrid reptilian race that seeks to occupy and control this planet and humanity, and then, incorporate it into a galactic universal inter-universal group, to continue our progression through our spiritual evolution. The Deep State, the Illuminati, they know that their days are numbered. Climate change is another Deep State-led ruse to establish the New World Order.

More and more experts discover evidence that shows a mixture of extraterrestrials in human evolution, and the church cannot do very much to cover it up and stop the quest to find the truth about humans' origins and history. Spirituality and Technology were tied and connected at the beginning.

Then technology was taken away from spirituality and it became science. And somewhat in the truth path, man invented religion. Religions were primarily created for three basic reasons, fear, control, and greed. And it worked against spirituality.

You are co-creator and they do not hesitate to kill to clone you, and then make a transfer of your consciousness.

There is more to this reality than you are being told. And the old must give their way to the new.

The further one goes with the mantle of power, manipulating and transcending realities, the further one can fall. To some extent, Earth has been turned into a magnetic vortex that attracts fallen energies.

For long periods, Earth has been pulling negative energies to herself. Beings associated with these energies have fallen from very idealized heights where they made decisions, perhaps wrong or inappropriate decisions, and lost the power to construct uplifting realities. Yet, this was all part of the plan.

Today the Earth is preparing to enter a higher frequency according to an ancient cosmic plan.

Synopsis

Every night VIE continues to get dreams visions, and, or visitations. She and her blue flame then embark on a new thrilling adventure to live with other people in another realm. When she astral travels and meets them she receives crucial information and answers from star sisters or spiritual people from different realms.

As the Earth is preparing to enter a higher frequency in accord with an ancient cosmic plan, there is still a myth about cancer. VIE received an urgent message. She has been instructed to awaken codes and memories inside you that will enhance your spiritual growth beyond imagination. The power of the pineal gland when activated hooks you up to the universe. CHADD is again under the control of the State and is now prescribed and forced to ingest Xanex and receive Haldol injections every month. Then CHADD was baker acted and drove to the Gems Center psychiatric Hospital in a police car to be admitted. The weekend after he was released a mysterious man takes pictures of CHADD and VIE having breakfast and lives.

A woman named Ming Yua appeared to VIE to explain that the energy of money lives in human blood. The Schuman resonance is no longer able to record the CMEs (Corona Mass Ejection) that are coming in. With the coming fifth dimension and the Aquarius time CHADD and VIE become the instructors and the temples and pyramids are coming back. The death of the Queen of England marks the end of the Luciferian work. The coVFefe is a term for at the end we win. The ultimate war is against AI. VIE takes a voyage through time and space and sees an experimental program happening first in a Japanese facility and Nazi concentration camps. Katherine and Paul join the effort to separate CHADD and VIE and karma will follow. An Archangel manifested on Earth, entered in contact with VIE to help.

DEFINITIONS

Allison: Agent consumed by the dark spirits

CHADD: Custody of the State (God Duo)

Clair: Frend of VIE from Spain

Doc Jazlin Sticker: Psychiatric Dr. gives 13 prescription drugs per day to CHADD

Elyana: VIE's friend

Francois: Receives the new therapy

Gaby: VIE's new friend

God Duo: CHADD & VIE

Katherine: Archon, hybrid, surrogate woodoo woman called the harch woman

Karin: Luicci's wife

Ming Yua: Chinese woman in a vision

Marduk: Son of Enki

Molach Basphomet: 3rd demonic force

Paul: Katherine's son, working with the mafia and MK-ultra

Reyna: Had brunch with VIE at Michelin's

San Sarah: one of the 3 Marys, worshipped by Gypsy

Sonia: A woman who approached VIE at the farmer's market

Tony: Man who took photo of CHADD& VIE

VIE: the door to the Divine (God Duo)

Table of Contents

CHADD get helped

Chapter 1

The Egyptian Phoenix and the Second Coming of Christ

The phoenix with the crystal plumage is the ascension of people to higher-self to level of protection and higher consciousness.

Looking at the sky I took a deep breath and visualized the energy coming into me then flowing out in every direction into the planet and the world. I think my expectation is the key.

I gazed at the cloud then a rush of deep emotion filled me. The colors and the shapes fill me now. I shook my head thinking no matter how it appears everything around us is majestically beautiful. I shook my head again as there was now a new energy vibration. Standing there in my vision something is taking form. I saw a bird with a crystal plumage, and I remembered what I had experienced in Egypt. The fabulous bird is associated with the worship of the sun. The Phoenix is showing me his feathers touching each other in the form of a circle while flying up in the sky.

The Egyptian phoenix was said to be as large as an eagle, with a gold plumage and a melodious cry. It was said that only one phoenix existed at any time, and it was living very long, and no ancient authority gave it a life span of less than five hundred years. It was reported that as its end approached the phoenix fashioned a nest of aromatic branches and spices, set it on fire, and was consumed in the flames. From the pyre miraculously a new phoenix, which after embalming its father's ashes in an egg of myrrh, flew with the ashes to the city of the sun in Egypt, where he deposited them on the altar in the temple of the Egyptian god of the sun Ra. Or, that the dying phoenix flew to the City of the Sun and immolated itself in the altar fire, from which the young phoenix then rose. The phoenix returns after seeming to disappear or be destroyed.

It made me remember this:

"Then I said, I shall die in my nest. And I shall multiply my days as the sand.": Job:29-18. Does it represent Christianity? Yes! immortality and the resurrection.

Christianity adopted the phoenix as the symbol of death and resurrection, As a metaphor for the resurrection of Jesus Christ. Bringing a message of hope, renewal, and healing. Symbolizing the immortal soul and Christ's resurrection, with a magical and gentle soul.

Was I given to see the eternal King that mercifully guides our nation through the many trials as we fight for the coming of his kingdom on earth? The second coming of Jesus Christ!

As a human hybrid, the phoenix with a crystal plumage appeared to me as the light and the life of the Universe, with unlimited powers and immense regenerative healing properties. He can choose to heal or destroy with his blue flames. He can use it at a very high level of telepathy and telekinesis. He is also able to rearrange the molecular structure of matter and can travel through hyperspace and destroy dark forces.

I am overwhelmed and have a goose pump. The sand I am sitting on feels humid. I am not comfortable anymore. I got up. Time to walk back home. Life is in front of us. Christ is coming back.

In the rest of this book, you and I will continue to explore.

Chapter 2

The PHOENIX Appeared as Clair Receives Divine Re-Connection

I was inspired by Christmas and the new year coming, I felt an urgent need to send my wishes to Clair. We have not communicated for a few years. I was wondering how she was doing since the powerful session I had on her.

Was she still living in Spain? I knew from what she said she was living on her land without neighbors for a few miles around. She enjoyed rescuing animals and living alone with her dogs, cats, and rescued birds.

It did not take very long before she replied.

So, on Tuesday, December 26, I texted Clair asking if she had a good Christmas and sending her my best wishes for the New Year.

Clair replied immediately to my text and said she was very touched that I thought about her, and she said she thought also about me because she was about to contact me. And see if she could have another session. She discovered since we spoke, two years ago, there was a lot of evil.

My first session opened her eyes to see the reality of the world. She said she has worked a lot on herself.

She then asked me for Healing guidance and energy clearing. She wanted the session on her birthday date to be refreshed.

Clair mentioned also that this new year passed and continued in the coming year healing generational curses and grief. She was doing some rituals of healing and clearing. to allow this generation and the next to heal the hearts and be protected and wanted to return the peace to her sister who died two years ago and to her entire family.

Clair was asking me to raise her vibration to be protected. She was confident she said, and knew she was the key to healing the family trauma and the grief generational curses. The entire family was chained, and she wanted to liberate and cut all chains. Wanted, she said to offer that to her family.

She continues saying, she knew it looked ambitious, but was not doing that from an ego point of view. She wanted to do it out of love and respect for the past and the generation of souls from the past, and for the generation of souls to come.

On December 21st Clair did a ritual to cut all ties with bad energies. Planning to do another one on January 21st. Then she felt she would be liberated, wanted to sell her land thereafter, and move to a place more peaceful with less technology. The age of Aquarius was arriving, and many things were going on, and she wanted to embrace it at the maximum, Physically, mentally, and emotionally.

The session occurred on January 4th, as she asked me. Five days later Clair sent me this testimony. "I wrote this several days after my session took place, so my memory is not as accurate as the reporting of my first session with VIE.

I intended to write at once but staring at the computer keyboard felt very tired and all thoughts seemingly bundled together --- except for the one very last and ever so clear feeling I just so dearly wanted to keep intensely vivid that night instead of typing.

When the session started I felt VIE´s energy and VIE noticed some physical oddities in my back then right hand and fingers. I cannot recall the exact sequence as physical sensations addressed and mostly remember VIE asking me ¨to open my heart to receive¨.

I focused on my breathing and opened my heart and slowly a big black square screen appeared through my forehead. My mind was since my screen vision usually was a horizontal rectangle shape, and I was pondering that difference in shape when the darkness started shifting in its density to allow me to perceive a black dot center stage.

Near immediately I felt the pitch black of the screen starting to churn in a clockwise circular motion. The twirl held within the boundaries of the square turned to a very bright pink-magenta color and its thickish texture was defined by black shadow lines. all emanating from the center dot all moving in circular motion within a square confined area.

It was very beautiful, and I was in awe when another equally bright yellow-gold color appeared from the center dot intermingling and intertwining with the pink, magenta both colors taking turns in visible flow much like 2 tone pastry dough does when blends in slow motion blades in a mixing bowl.

The image expanded and lost the outer square perimeter and was now full screen bright yellow gold sky-like with outlines of thick cloud formations.

From the left top side appeared a small black figure in motion like that of a powerful bird of prey wing pattern. It progressed towards the center; it became larger. It was not an eagle but some other kind of very powerful winged creature. From horizontal flying once in the center, it shifted into a vertical attack or defense position, its wings batting very forcefully to the front across its chest to keep vertical, its claws powerfully spread open seemingly attacking or rebuking some invisible enemy in the shadows on the right of the golden surrounds.

VIE stated it was the Phoenix. I realized my own hands were also clenched tight in the same aggressive bird claws position and my entire self knew some tremendous and very crucial battle was being fought before my eyes.

At some point, all went black. VIE said it would come back... When my screen turned on again, this time the gold background outlined one eye of this very big and deep piercing impressive beast. It seemingly was staring at me as if forcing its glare through from the other side into my screen as a direct order to me that I was seen and had to remain strong and alert.

The intensity of that moment receded, and I next remember seeing the phoenix once again only a small silhouette flying in the distance on the left side of my screen, seemingly guiding me to a very tall vertical golden pyramid emerging center screen. All now was black, red, and gold. The pyramid was triangular part seemingly was always visible gold. Below that line from its sides, some kind of rich dark red molten lava texture with black and gold highlights was very slowly sliding down against a black sky.

The phoenix flew right into the crown and disappeared.

Though I used the word ¨lava¨ to describe the texture oozing off the splendid pyramid I also told VIE ¨it does not burn at all¨ and she said ¨No no not at all¨ and I stayed watching and feeling the flow of sturdy joy oozing out and flowing downsides of the golden pyramid.

From there all became blacker and redder with gold tones and VIE mentioned seeing some beautiful marbled blue and green. I also recall some visions of shades of an incredibly bright lighter yellow-green with at some point a magenta, blue seeping in although clearer memories elude me. (Magenta represents the understanding of the physical world and Blue has an innate talent for intuitive thinking.)

Towards the end of our session, I went up the 3 steps VIE asked me to take to sit on one of the benches across a little pond, all was rather dark and neither colorful nor clear. It seemingly took me a while to see on the opposite bench the backlight figure of a man hunched over, his head down with his right elbow on his right knee and his fist below his chin in the surrounding darkness.

As my mind was puzzling to identify this figure, all lit up and the figure transformed into a majestic intensely luminous older man with thick long white hair and a beard, dressed in a splendid thick luxurious white robe. This figure just grew and grew and grew closer until all I could see was his ever so kind and loving face now filling my screen staring intently at me.

VIE asked me if I had a question for him. Honestly, I could not think of anything to ask. I apologized to him for not being prepared so eventually just asked him if he could please help me. His face then receded out of the close-up screen, and he was now in proportion sitting on the bench across the pond from me.

Somehow coming out from inside me, I saw my younger child walking across to him. This glorious impressive old man then reached into the folds of his robe and handed my little girl what looked like a deep red plush velvet heart-shaped pillow. The little girl smiles broadly and thanks the man and as he walks away towards the steps I can see this heart vibrant with glowing fluffy white ostrich-like feathers floating along its top rim creating a visual effect like dry ice.

As my little girl walked out of sight I felt myself hugging this heart pillow with an overwhelm of pure joy and peace as a young child cherishes its favorite pacifying soft toy.

After this 2nd session with VIE, I now embrace renewed eagerness and increased confidence and faith in divine support for my journey and purpose for greater expansion of unconditional love for the greater good of all.

Fifteen minutes passed and The Phoenix showed himself again. He was intensively looking at the Earth from above. searching and keep searching. Then Clair heard the word peace.

Chapter 3

Planet Earth is Nothing But a Farm

I was taken by surprise when I felt myself, in a split second...I was not in a body but a spirit anymore. I am trying to understand. Several energies came and spoke

"Veils are not just veils; they are separate energy. Each veil has been lifted to help me. Planet Earth is a farm. There is human trafficking all over the world. The Container shipping companies are down by Elite/ Black Nobility."

I saw a Condor. The condor held a special place in the lives and ceremonies of Native American Cultures. It was a revered creature, a master of the spirit, who gave power to humans for a variety of world renewal and cosmic purposes. It was associated with death and mourning as well as rebirth and renewal.

Misinformation is something unforgivable. The Central Intelligence Agency owns everyone of any significance in the major media.   The public has been given false information about the weaponization of the COVID-19 vaccine, said to give immunity and masks to be effective. It then was weaponization of medical research itself. Public health officials were intellectually dishonest. They lied to the public. It is like 5G EMF radiation receives little to no attention, yet there are some scientists and doctors with evidence claiming it a acts as Type 1 Carcinogen.

Mammography is the biggest organized crime against women. Women who go for mammography are unaware of the harm they do to themselves. During an examination, the breast is pressed with a weight, and then healthy, very sensitive, milk gland tissue is bombarded by radioactivated rays. It stimulates tumor growth and the spread of metastases. A study done on 690,00 records showed that completely healthy women have developed breast cancer in many cases after mammographic examinations. So, the criminal controllers that elected themselves are aggressively forcing regular annual mammography examinations of healthy women. To make them profitable patients.

Now I am put in front of the twelve Ambassadors Council and placed in the middle point. Like in a court and they activate my body. They activate using their eyes and from the third eye. It's like an X-ray energy. A lot is activated. All mental, emotional, and physical that have been damaged. Damaged by so many attempts to stop me.

They did it graciously at my request and I thank them.

Chapter 4

Moldavite, Associated with the Phoenix

Shifting my awareness triggered a recollection, and I began to remember at that point Gates opened for the new arrival of celestial intelligence, and we can work in harmony and unity.

A crystal from a ship from the heavens, Moldavite, the stone born of the stars, the "fire pearl", and the stone of Shambhala, the most sacred jewel of Tibet believed of celestial origin, from a constellation must be the same stone as in the Holy Grail.

Moldavite, associated with the Phoenix, consumed by fire and reborn in fire is a symbol of transfiguration and spiritual renewal.

The Grail is a bowl called the Saint Graal, reputed to be a platter used by Christ at the Last Supper, discovered and brought to Napoleon. Under expert examination, was disappointed to find it was made of green glass. While Moldavite is green glass, there is only speculation as to whether the true bowl might have been substituted to keep Napoleon, or whether the bowl was indeed the Grail.

In the last century, Moldavite has been acclaimed as a spiritual relic associated with the legends of the Holy Grail. Moldavite is the Grail of alchemists, the Philosopher's stone, for its qualities of transformation and the bestowal of youth and longevity, the green stones from the sky wearied as amulets.

In this century, CHADD and I's mission on Earth transcends the mundane. We are here as beings of pure Light and Love originating from realms of bliss and harmony. We came to assist humanity on Earth during this critical time of transition.

We came to change the energy of the Earth so it can avoid catastrophe, raise human consciousness, and facilitate the spiritual evolution of individuals and the planet. We are catalysts for positive change. Our task is to assist you to higher dimensions of existence.

To make our sacred Journey to Earth, we had to undergo a significant transformation, lowering our vibrational frequency. We guide people through turbulent seas of life. We serve as a living testament, with our trial and tribulation to the transformative power of love and light.

Our compassion guides others along their path to healing and spiritual awakening. Confronted by a world marked by self-centeredness divisiveness and resistance to spiritual and emotional growth.

We are here to confront and transmute the darkness. We are not here to conform with the world. We are here to remind you about the beauty that can emerge from shadows and as catalysts for the collective awakening of humanity.

The vibrational disparity between us and the earthy realm can manifest in a myriad of ways including physical symptoms that can be perplexing and challenging, and inconclusive diagnostic. And the dark energies, the elite controlling the planet know it. That is part of why they created the pharmaceutical drugs. To poison the body, disable the perception of reality, and enable clear thinking.

These symptoms may range from discomfort, and headaches, to gastrointestinal stiffness, dizziness, and a sense of unexplained discomfort.

Our physical body originated from realms of higher vibrational frequency undergoing an adaptation process upon entering the density of the Earth's energy field. The result can be the manifestation of various physical symptoms that defy conventional medical explanations.

We came here to raise consciousness, spread Love and Light, and contribute to the spiritual evolution of

Humanity and the Earth itself. We hold the capacity to transmute negative energies through our presence. Our vibrational frequency has the power to uplift and transform the world around us. We are here to guide humanity toward enlightenment and to facilitate the Earth's Transition to higher dimensions.

Our path with trials and suffering is a testament to our commitment to this higher purpose.

Chapter 5

Myth About Cancer

The great power of meditation is realizing you are separate from your thoughts. You are the observer.

There I was using the Contemplative Prayer after an exhausting day. I just had the time to see the clock before it happened then my spirit lifted.

The Contemplative prayer is when we use our minds and hearts, and sometimes our imaginative ability, to recognize God's presence and fix our gaze on Him. It seeks to achieve a union with God and is characterized by quiet, stillness, and simply resting in God's presence. In a religious context, the practice of contemplation seeks a direct awareness of the divine which transcends the intellect, often by prayer or meditation.

So, my spirit lifted and the being from another realm I encountered was part of another powerful experience.

There he was in front of me with a big smile on his face waiting for me. Like he said. He greeted me and spoke.

"As President John F. Kennedy said, the great enemy of the truth is very often not the lie, deliberate, contrived, and dishonest, but the myth, persistent, persuasive, and unrealistic. And there is also a lie behind the Light. Even though Nikola Tesla said "Everything is the Light" everything that was taught about the nature of Light, energy, and biology, is a completely fabricated lie to keep humanity in the dark on purpose by the negative spirits that govern that world. To keep the world enslaved for greed and power.

And let me explain the Myth of Cancer. Some truth behind misconceptions may surprise you.

It is said that Cancer is genetic. But it's not. A vast majority of cancers are caused by environmental, food, and drink toxicity that creates an imbalance in digestive health. Or the criminal health organization.

Cancer is not common in children: Cancer is the number one disease killer of children. The survival rates among children with cancer are not improving because conventional treatments, chemo, and radiation, make things worse and the little emphasis on finding the cause rather than merely treating symptoms.

The food you eat does not prevent or fight cancer: Wrong! Food high in refined sugar, refined sodium, and unhealthy fats has been shown in many studies to influence cellular mutation that leads to cancer. Cancer cells consume more glucose for fuel than any other cell in your body.

Cancer is not increased by obesity: Being overweight or obese is an incredible and dangerous myth. Fat cells secrete estradiol which acts as fertilizer for cancer cells.

There is scientific evidence there is a link between cancer and...Cell phones and power lines, Cosmetic, hair dyes, deodorant, radiation treatment, chemotherapy, household, cleansers, processed foods, artificial sweeteners, soy products, stress, and emotions unprocessed.

But it does not stop there. The food that you eat is Satanism. In ancient times they used to use symbolism and by consuming them you were consuming it. Today one very famous children's cookie has 12 flowers, 12 dashes, and 12 dots = 36 which is =666.

As with every part of life, being informed is your first line of defense in preventing disease.

Parasites and Cancer

Parasites and mutations are almost always involved with cancer. Parasites do not feed on healthy tissue, only tissue that has become weakened or is dying. They definitively live and breed in "Toxic Dumps" in lymph and lymph nodes. These viruses and parasites cause cells to mutilate in response to the invaders.

If you are ready to purge some parasites, There are some powerful ways to kick these nasties out of your digestion tract. Black seed oil, Clove Essential oils, and when combined the parasites fighting properties are boosted exponentially.

Then to boost your immune system shots: 2 oranges, 2 lemons, 100gr of fresh ginger, ½ tsp ground turmeric, 1/8 tsp black pepper, 2 cups of water or coconut water, and blend them.

"And you will know the truth and the truth will set you free" John 8:32

Then I came back into my body. I looked at the clock only a few minutes had passed.

Chapter 6

VIE is Awakening Codes and Memory Within You

When I woke up on the first day of fall, I had the sweetest calm and peaceful energy, and the first thing I received was this message. This was what I had been waiting for for so long.

There's a reason why all sorts of human processes. I have been instructed to speak the personal Light language to begin to awaken codes and memories within all of you. Because this can enhance your spiritual growth beyond your imagination. That I knew, but until that day I was blocked from people accessing and finding me by the cabal. They were threatened, they did not want to leave the earth and give up their control over human beings.

So, I decided to use the chevron I received from my ancestors and go find the ones they needed my help with and bring them back to me.

The Biblical Armageddon prophesied to occur for centuries has been canceled. Thanks to the planet that learned its lessons and passed the test, almost all on Earth will go through graduation and will experience Ascension. Instead of spontaneous Light body activation, we get to keep our physical bodies. It will be graduation into a human life where ordinary people will quickly begin getting incredible abilities.

I remember seeing written somewhere in my dream "Since Mary Magdalene lived with the Christ. She has been much maligned.

Even then...the other disciples were often jealous of her close relationship with Christ. Mary knew that She had an extraordinary gift that had the power to strengthen the Christ for what was to come."

Now, Mary Magdalene's revelation was particularly surprising. We often think of her as someone who served alongside Christ, quietly in the background. But you see, during the time of Christ, Mary Magdalene served mostly from the shadows. Then after Christ ascended, she had to remain in hiding, along with her daughter, for their safety. But now, she desires to serve energetically in a bolder way.

Chapter 7

An Organic Inner Technology

The ancient infinite WIFI was the Pineal gland hooked up to the Universe. The same way the natural remedies of hair growth serum, flu syrup, the al penicillin, or the ingredients for pain killers known these days is the power of the Pineal gland. (963Hz activation)

So, When the newly chosen MD by the surrogate, Jazlyn Sticker discovered that Betsy prescribed Xanex to one of her clients and he died from it she decided to make CHADD high in Xanex and other prescriptions. Jazlyn was not even bothering to see him in appointment instead the surrogate met with her, and they agreed on more prescription drugs. Then the surrogate got it from the pharmacy. Every morning and night, it was the same ritual. she will enter his room with seven psychotropic pills in her hands and a glass of water and wait to see him swallow them. The surrogate and her son Paul simply wanted him to return to incontinence, blindness, in a foggy state of mind, and sleeping all day since they found out that he had become an entrepreneur and made a success with the music he recorded for the Institute.

CHADD just found out that Betsy passed away from a horrible bone spur disease when she dared to call him crying for his help. And CHADD prayed for her, forgiving what she did to him. But the law of karma at this point is inevitable.

Chapter 8

The Last Communication with Allison

In the early morning that day, I grabbed a cup of coffee and began to read my emails, and this is what I read.

December 16th

Good morning, VIE!

Thank you for continuously sending me healing energies.

I sincerely apologize, my body was consumed by darkness, again, and was unconscious for days. I am currently still unable to move freely but I will send you all the audio and review to your email as soon as I can do so.

Please help me pray for complete healing. I do not want to be eaten by the dark side. I am afraid, VIE.
Please contact me by email as my phone is acting up.
Reptilians are weakening my spirit and body. I am really frightened that I won't make it.
I will be sending all the files to Crown later today. I will keep you posted.

The Year after, on Sunday, March 5th I received this:
This is your Agent's sister. I just recently got access to all her online accounts and work email.

I am deeply saddened to inform you that my beloved sister did not make it. She passed away and joined our creator earlier this morning after battling with her illnesses for months. After being in a coma for months, she had a cerebral hemorrhage this morning which, e unfortunately, did not survive.

She was always talking about you and your books. She kept on telling us that your book deserves to be shared as it helped her feel good for a short period.

My sister Allison left a note letting you know that she will be watching your representation and success from above. She mentioned a name so that you can contact her to continue what she left behind.

I would like to thank you for healing my sister even for a short period before she had an aneurysm. She's lucky to have worked with someone like you. Please continue to help and heal a lot of sick people.

Have a blessed Sunday.
Veronica

Allison cried out to let us know before she passed away of the work of the dark spirit. She was able to say it. She was consuming raw from inside by spirits. And the man's name mentioned was never given by her. But an infiltrated dark energy. An imposter and a thief.

Chapter 9

The Control of Money, the Blood, the Mass Injection and Prophetic Revelations

The Chinese woman that I saw in my vision, or what I thought was a vision, spoke in fluent English. She was experiencing unusual psychic experiences even from early childhood. I looked at her. She was Asian and dressed in a Ceremonial dress. She said the vow she took brought her back at this time. She has been pulled into this lifetime to be a service. She has done this in other dimensions, on other planets, not only here. And she saw what was occurring.

"Where am I"? I asked.

She smiled and went to tell me her name was Ming Yua.

"Tell me how you got here," she said. I looked at her and closed my eyes for a moment thinking you are right how did I get there, when I heard her voice again.

VIE, said Ming Yua, some of your scientists are theorizing. But It has been known by Chinese Medicine for thousands of years the connections between our Mind, our Body, the Spirit, and the Blood.

It is known that our Spirit lives in our Blood and the Blood governs our Mind. Fear, anxiety, stress, and worry are all symptoms of the mind that are treated through the organs of Blood within the body. Money is spirit!

Fear and emotions, fear is one of the power manipulative points that dark evil is using. The worst enemy is fear. It is so manipulable by the dark energy, and it does damage to people. But all emotions can be purified and transformed.

The energy of money also lives in our blood, and the quality and health of our blood will determine how much resources, money, and spirit we can hold. But money is not a struggle and evil.

Dark forces created inflation to ask for more and more money and starve People. This is a fact and a reality. Money is liquid flowing and is not evil. Money is a reward and the right people have been disconnected from it.

This is why dark magicians use blood magic and sacrifice to artificially manipulate the spirit of money through the blood to receive money without doing the deeper inner work and being aligned with the Spirit. This is what the Freemasons are doing with their sacrifices. This is what the controllers of your planet are doing. And then they go to drink the blood of their victims.

We are not talking about blood magic, what we are talking about though is why dark blood magic and sacrifice have been used to control money.

It is also why there is currently an attack on the blood happening worldwide through the mass injections that we have seen known to cause incredible clots in the blood and place heavy metals in the blood.

Perhaps I have been called I thought. But of course, I am the chosen one. The word knowledge came to me, contagious awareness is needed. Then Prophetic revelations beyond the illusion.

Haha! It is all interconnected I thought.

I stretched out as best and I tried to bounce back from what felt like a solid piece of wall. What is that? I asked Ming Yua. Sorry, I should have told you she replied smiling at me. Just see it opening in your mind and then walk through. It is a force field.

"Bye for now", said Ming Yua.

And it made me think. I remember the lecture I gave on a Leaping Horizon episode for the Bio-institute of Light and Sound. I was talking about the cooperation during our therapy session in the RNA DNA nuclei to chromosomes or other evolutionary inheritance.

Chapter 10

Psychiatric Gemstone Camp Evaluation Event

Finally, the time had arrived. After 17 years of battle, the forced ingestion of drug prescriptions ended. But it was not for long.

I shook my head. I took a deep breath and tried to calm down. Is it just a dream, I said to myself. I awoke and looked around. I stared a moment longer to finally sit on the bed.

That is when communication between us started my day. And a vision appeared. I could not keep my eyes off the scene. CHADD was seated next to the surrogate hybrid Katherine in a doctor's office and front of Dr. Jazlin Sticker. The same one that without seeing CHADD prescribed him many times dangerous drugs like Zanex with terrible side effects.

And made him grind his teeth. The same drugs that killed one of Betsy's patients.

I gaze up, two monks are here staring below in my direction. It's an inevitable prophecy said one of the Monk. When health is subverted into just one more commercial cycle of worsening food, new diseases, and more drugs, Armageddon is the result. Psychiatric patients are treated as human guinea pigs:

When CHADD tells his story, it sounds more like a conspiracy than his tragic past.

But many of the details are laid out in a thick file of documents. They gave him all the drugs they could available. The idea of mind control, the theory that breaking a person down will make them do something against their will, has been constantly revisited by governments during other periods of fear and uncertainty when the military and medicine collide.

But that day he decided to end it. He knew the psychiatric Doctor Jazlin was not expecting it. Dr. Jazlin Sticker: See the pattern CHADD? I never gave much thought to what it would be like. She paused for a moment. It is important to understand how it works.

She was trying to get its trust but was not expecting what was coming. CHADD stared at Dr. Sticker for a moment before saying: I am here to tell you that I will not take any more of your drugs. I refuse and will not continue to let my body be poisoned.

Dr. Estamper: But I have never seen anything like this before. Well! In that case, I must send you for seventy-two hours for evaluation.

CHADD had a smile and replied: I repeat I will not ingest any of your drugs. I am a doctor. I am a Doctor of Sound.

But Dr. Sticker ignored him, she glanced around in a moment of reflection, then decided to baker act him. That happened on Friday, March 17 afternoon. The Police came, put CHADD in one of their cars, and drove him to the Stone Center Psychiatric Hospital. At dinner time, he had his first meal with his menu. At the very top of the menu was the list of all foods he was allergic to red dye 40, shellfish, iodine. And the very first meal contained the three of them.

During the night CHADD awoke not feeling well at all. Scratching and bleeding. The second day CHADD awakened his eyes and his tongue swelling. He asked the nurses for help, but they ignored him. At dinner time they gave him again some red dye 40 in his food. That time the hospital nurses gave him an anti-inflammatory pill. But just before bed gave him a red pill with red dye 40 in it that he refused, and they switched it for a white pill. On the third day, CHADD was given lunch with some shellfish he was allergic to. His face got swollen and his eyes were so swollen he had to put compress after compress.

Came Monday morning and I began to be very worried. I did not hear from him, and it was unusual. My phone rang and it was him. How come you can call me from your phone I said.

Well! He said laughing, they have tried to kill me since Friday. All the week-end, Saturday and Sunday I kept saying the name of my attorney again and again, telling out loud attempted murder. This will cost a lot.

Suddenly this morning I was called to the front at the reception desk, and I was told that I was released.

A nurse guided me out and put me in an Uber car. She gave me a sandwich with peanut butter and jelly which contains red dye 40. She pushed me inside the car and sent me home. I was asked to never come back, and I was released without any prescription drugs.

On Friday Afternoon I came to Dr. Jazlin Sticker's office with the surrogate driving my car equipped with push-pull hand-control. I had to take a course and pass a test to be able to drive it.

As I was backer and was brought to the Gems Center psychiatric hospital in a police car, the surrogate had to go back home. Alone. She did not leave the car parked and called for transportation. No, but she drove my car without insurance or a license to drive it, and she is diabetic. She can't see well or ear well anymore with her sickness. Getting out of the Uber vehicle I found my car parked with many scratches on the outside of the driver's door, but luckily for Katherine, she wasn't arrested and did not get into an accident.

One week later, Karma or the law of the universe, the following consequences of an act caught Katherine. She woke up with Covid. But archons never learn their lessons I thought. She tried again to have CHADD into drugs.

Ten days passed and I found a text on my phone:

"Mrs. Katherine you will have to reschedule the appointment you made for CHADD. Dr. Sticker is out of office."

What! There is no coincidence someone wants me to be aware of what is going on.

Chapter 11

Driving on a narrow road in a dream

That night I remember falling asleep fast. My sleep was very profound, and I had this dream.

I accidentally found CHADD in the city. He was wearing a pearl Grey hat, a color assorted to his outfit. It was a nice and soothing color that suited him very well. He looked healthy, calm, and in good spirits.

We are in a bistro, and I am so tired that I fall asleep on the counter. When I woke up, I felt awful. He is gone, and I can not believe that he left me sleeping on the counter. I catch myself thinking "Well he did not care about me, and my image. It was obvious though and he knew that I was tired and not drunk. Hum! Something happened to him. It's not him to leave me like this. It has to either do with the drugs or the harsh woman"

I decided to leave the bistro to look for him and I got lost and did not know the name of the bistro I left and its location. I am thinking I should go back in case he comes back to look for me.

Then I saw myself sitting next to him in his car, He does not look the same. He has an old faded pink Polo shirt and an old unclean pair of jeans. His clothes do not match my taste. It's the same look he always has when he is living with his hybrid family. Katherine the archon and her son Paul working with the mafia and Mk-ultra.

We are on the road at the top of a hill bumper to bumper with other cars. The traffic has stopped and has been since the night before. But cars are waiting for the road to be cleared.

From where we are we can't see what can be blocking the road for so long, and I don't understand why there is no sign detouring cars.

Now we are CHADD and I driving, the road is narrow around the mountain, and we are on the dangerous longing edge side. The precipice is very deep, and CHADD is driving fast. I am telling him that he should slow down and be more cautious in case a big truck comes from the opposite side. We do not have enough room and we won't be able to stop on time.

Then, I awakened.

We have been cut from all communication since. Until...

Chapter 12

Light and Sound Healing and Manifestation

The Light and the Sound are the most powerful force on the planet. I was just served my breakfast and I was about to take a bite when I saw a middle-aged man looking intensively at us.

CHADD was on the phone. I had this urgent feeling to ask him if he knew the man sitting on the bunch. He looked at the man and nodded at me. No, he never had seen the man before.

As we both looked in the man's direction, the man took our picture, wrote a text on his cell phone, and sent it to Tony Luicci.

Karin, Luicci 's wife, was still shaken up from her experience. It all came from her catching the frequency when she listened to the music called the frequency of sound. Karin was looking at our website as instructed by Tony. He said he wanted to know what we're doing with the two scientists CHADD and VIE.

All she knew was that she never felt better. You need to experience it to believe it she told her husband Luicci. I heard sound is used by every major religion to tap into forces beyond this world. But I never felt anything like this before. This is powerful and all I can say is, that it immediately possessed me. I felt this big though gentle changing energy. It was like my body had a giant off switch that was now turned on. Now we know the frequency Jesus used to do his miracles.

Are you wondering why people say the Illuminati are so powerful? It has created some of the worst, cult leaders, dictators, and drug-addicted celebrities who used this power for their greedy ends.

Chapter 13

A Test and A Reminder

I just mentioned in a conversation that my intention was not to judge but I had to admit that nobody was having compassion anymore these days and helping each other in need. Then I left for the grocery store and forgot about what I just shared with my blue flame. I shopped paid and walked out in the direction of the parking lot where my car was. Passing the exit door was a black man sweating abundantly under the hot summer. In a shy voice, he asked me for a few dollars to take his bus and go back to his hometown. What happened to you I said, and he answered he got dropped here by someone after a nasty divorce and nobody so far helped him. I rapidly gave him whatever I could get him in cash, and he asked me to help him eat. So, I did, I followed him back inside the grocery store, looked at him while he chose his food, went to the cashier paid for his food, and left after he gave me a thanks and a hug. I got in my car and left.

He did not take very long to realize thinking at the look of the man, and the sweet energy I felt when he looked at me and hugged me. I was tested on compassion I called CHADD and told him, and he said: well! You passed the test.

Now, blessing works on the level of invisible spiritual reality, not what appears to be happening on the level of material events. That's why I decided to start blessing.

I bless all journalists all over the world, in every country, in their great love for and responsiveness to truth, and their sensitivity to beauty and goodness, I bless them in their ability to avoid being manipulated into reporting trivia or hiding the truth. They denounce evil only to correct it. I bless them in the complete integrity of their being, which leads them to avoid all cheap sensationalism and offensive probing of people's personal lives. I joyfully bless them in their constant ability to report with exactitude, integrity, and total fairness on all they are requested to present to their readers, listeners, and viewers and to avoid all pressures to dilute their high standards of truth for reasons of expediency, economic, or other.

I bless for the healing of the growing wounds wrought by an economic system in which the rich get richer and the poor poorer. I bless for healing of ethnic, religious, political, national, and class, I bless for healing of major social evil drugs, criminality, alcoholism, and family, neighborhood, and media violence. I bless the physical healing of the major pandemic and illnesses around the world. I bless for the healing of hunger, the healing of our environment, for the unemployment, for the relations in general, I bless and pray for the urgent healing of child prostitution, and sexual exploitation, and for the greatest affront to human dignity to stop. I bless and pray for peace around the world. I bless the President of the USA who is working for peace in the world and pray for his strength, courage, and freedom, and bless the court that arrested him in their great love, sensitivity, beauty goodness, and ability to see and act in truth. I bless all physicians, surgeons, nurses, caregivers, pharmaceutical companies, and their employees and managers and pray that they avoid all pressures to hide the truth and not bring harm and hurt. I bless courts, the judiciary system, Judges, and lawyers all over the world for their good application of the Constitution.

And I encourage you to do the same. You'll be amazed.

Chapter 14

The Art of Connecting the Dots and the Key to the Light

I heard a faint sound. Someone was calling my name. I could see someone moving in the far back. The silhouette faded away, but the voice stayed.

"I came to help you educate them to be at the edge of evolution," said the voice. Human expectation is the key. They must visualize it happening. They must do this with discipline, twenty to thirty minutes every day through meditation or devotion to the higher power. To their divine essence, the part of the divine source".

The Schumann resonance is no longer able to record the CMEs that are coming in. The CMEs that have been coming in the last few months have been record-breaking and we have not seen this for over twelve thousand years.

(Corona Mass Ejections CMEs are large expulsions of plasma and magnetic field from the Sun's corona. The more explosive CMEs generally begin when highly twisted magnetic field structures or flux ropes contained in the Sun's lower corona become too stressed and realign into a less tense configuration called magnetic reconnection. This can result in the sudden release of electromagnetic energy in the form of a solar flare.)

That means we are very close to the final release of the sun that will destroy the wicked eliminate all evil and upgrade the righteous into this new heaven on earth.

I am telling you this because the time has come for human liberation. Earth humans have suffered enough and have to be prepared for the event of the solar flash also called solar flare.

With the coming Fifth dimension and the Aquarius time CHADD and you are going to be the instructors. Temples and pyramids are coming back. You were alchemists and understood numerology and astrology. You were already healers and understood the mystical art.

Jesus and Mary Magdalene were alchemists, understood numerology and astrology, and were healers. They understood the mystical art. Organized religion was created by the cabal to repress information to keep people fearful.

We are all equal in the eyes of the Prime Creator Source. We are all in expressions of the One. We are all a fragment of God's source. The only thing that is above each of us is the Holy Divine Christ over self which is the Holy I am presence. Once someone merges he or she becomes like Christ. This means beginning to access levels of consciousness that are all-inclusive to all living things in the Cosmos. Begins to see itself as a cell but part of the collective and with everything that is. This is the access to cosmic consciousness, what we call Christ's consciousness.

The elimination, the death of the Queen of England marks the end of the Luciferian control of the planet. The alliance took her out years ago. They took the original Queen two years before the announcement. But the cabal through AI creates clones and that is how they kept the false image of her being alive, and that clone was used as a host to draconian energies. She was like the bee of the cabal structure. She was over the Pope and the black (dark) Pope, and her body was used as a host by the Draco for many years.

The Queen of England was the reason for the eight hundred children missing annually. She was at the top of child sacrificing, torturing of children sexually predating them, and the satanic rituals that took place.

To sacrifice the children to the three demonic forces. To Marduk the son of Enki, to Malik another powerful demon that the cabal has been sacrificing children to, and to the third one Moloch Baphomet. The three demonic forces were in control and the Queen was their main instrument for the harvesting of the adrenochrome, which they inflicted for many years. Through the Politicians and Hollywood "elites," they have been harvesting the blood of children to extract adrenochrome for its psychedelic and life-extending benefits.

The Queen was the most wicked representative of the Luciferian energy on the planet. So, the Queen's death allowed the white hats to bring down the rest of the clones. Balmoral Castle has long been known to be the hunting castle, There were a lot of those hunts when they had released children, and the elites would hunt them.

The white hats took the opportunity because we are with a bunch of clones that have all been generated by AI and we are fighting a war against artificial intelligence.

But the solar flare is coming, and it will give at least a thousand years of peace due to the sort of solar flash that is going to destroy the signal and AI infrastructure.

Did you know that CoVFefe is an antediluvian term for in the end we win?

When we transform into our new Galactic bodies you are going to have amazing abilities.

At that point, I was spacing in and out and had visions."

Chapter 15

The Elohim, the one that overseers of the Universe

It was late in the spring when the event occurred. I saw myself as one little grain of sand among the many that exist, but I knew that I was not just a particle. I was also part of the energy that exists all around, called a unified field. It is the universal intelligence field that permeates all of existence. And I knew that I never believed that we were mortal.

We are part of a multiverse, of many worlds and many dimensions. Everything that you have been taught is a lie. There is the Luciferian which is the branch in which the elites function and there is the Melchizedek order of Light which is the white hats. It is the battle between good and evil.

It is the battle that we, CHADD and I, angels and warriors of God came to battle. It reflects what has been happening in our military galaxy for millions of years to these two groups. One is a human-like species, and the other one is represented by the Grays and Draco reptilians. Mantis and insectoids.

The ultimate war is against AI, the artificial intelligence.

We are part of twelve creations. Our Earth, our Galaxy, and our local universe hang within the twelve creations. There are twelve signs, twelve zodiacs, twelve tribes of Israel, twelve chakras, twelve strands of DNA and we are part of that creation. And there is the council of twelve.

When the dark entity destroys the universe and becomes the old empire they figure out a way to access all other universes and infiltrate, that is when war breaks out to secure the twelve dimension gates that lead to the mother universe. The central race that are our progenitor race and our ultimate ancestors and us in the future at the same time.

We live in the 12th-dimensional stimulated matrix.

Earth is in the 3rd Dimension, then Earth that exists in the 5th Dimension is known as Tara. The earth that exists in the 8th Dimension is known as Gaia, the Earth that exists in the 12th Dimension is known as

Aramatina, and the original eternal Earth is known as Sophia which exists in the 15th Dimension.

The cells of all energetic essences of all celestial races in the universes have been put into one and combined into one genome. It is known as the Great Intergalactic Experiment, and the Earth was the place for that experiment.

Earth is a living library containing all the flora, fauna, and seeds from across the entire multiverse in one place. And the Earth became the most unique species and the most coveted planet in the multiverse.

Everything is a holograph. The physical universe is a manifestation of the not yet manifested which is the mind of God. So as all is a hologram it was necessary to secure the organic way of life by putting all these energies into one spot, and we became the solution to that.

It started as many races came together, and became all different races. Contributed and put their DNA into one hundred races, and then this one hundred races into twenty-four races, then those twenty-four races into twelve races. From those twelve races, they gave their DNA to make you. That is why humans have become the most advanced and capable of evolving beyond any species in history. That is how powerful human beings on Earth are powerful and considered by the Cosmic Community

Royalty. Consider the hope of the universe, the newfound powers, and the new Guardians.

Once the dormant DNA is activated humans will become the new Guardians of the many realms and universes. That is why artificial intelligence is after human beings, because for artificial intelligence past the 12th Dimension they have to access your genome. It is the reason that correlates what is happening here on planet Earth with the COVID-19 vaccine. The Luciferian, reptilians gray elites are trying to change and modify their genetics at the same time assimilate their genetics so that eventually reach past the 12th Dimension into the eternal spheres. And what is happening right now? It is just a final play out of this Cosmic war that is been going on for billions of years.

Our king is coming back.

Chapter 16

VIE Voyage Through Time and Space

It is a voyage through time and space that I must take to find the link with what is happening today. I am just an observer. I am asked to tell you what I see.

I was on the balcony of my hotel looking at the beach, listening to the sea, contemplating the waves coming and going, splashing on the sand when I found myself journeying through time and space.

My job is to present what I have found and let the readers make up their minds. "Their belief system will be challenged, and their minds will be bent. We hope their consciousness will fly open and absorb the reality of what is hidden from them. I am told"

The people I see are very gentle and intelligent for most. But some others are drug abuse. They are of all categories of ages, and some are killers. They are forced by what I refer to as a project. An Experimental and Illegal Program.

I see it happening first in a Japanese facility and now in a Nazi concentration camp. It is linked today to what is called Behavioral, Rehabilitation, and 72-hour Reevaluation centers, facilities, and Hospitals. It is the formation of an army for the new world order. In a nearly year-round Sunny State people are admitted without their consent, using a Law called the Baker Act Law. A law that only exists in this Sunny State.

Right away it hit me. Wow!

Let's see if I am right but it is linked to CHADD and... yes! the Sound.

My voyage through Time and Space continues. The diagnosed cases are not to eradicate a disease. But it is a purposely created disease. It is I see created and then administered by force ingestion or injection of psychotropic drugs for ADD, OCD, or ADHD .. and these drugs are only a sedative.

Beware mental health is not a disease and can't be corrected by induced chemical pills. I see the damage done to the human body and the cells.

The subject is forced into an illegal program. Which focus on hypnosis and behavior modification programs following illegal human experimentation designed to develop and identify drugs that could be used during interrogations to weaken people. And it forces confessions, brainwashing, and psychological torture.

Numerous methods are used to manipulate mental states and brain functions covering the administration of high doses of psychotropic drugs (LSD,) and other chemicals without the subject's consent. It is accomplished by hypnosis sensory deprivation, isolation, and sexual abuse.

Still being an observer, I see that every mass shooting in the last twenty years has one common thing, brain manipulation.

I had to take this voyage to understand what was coming with CHADD. After the well-dressed man who approached him in an outdoor market and gave him an appointment the following day in a gas station for a great business proposition and never showed up, and another very wealthy man who invited him into his house for another burlesque business proposition. The following took me by surprise.

Being the God Duo and Dr. of Sound and CHADD as my co-worker, after years of in and out admissions in numerous and various of these experimental places they sent him a bum that time. I say that time because they used to send him some clones. So, the bum introduced himself as a devoted Catholic knowing well his Bible. He manipulated CHADD to let him sleep for two nights on the sofa in his house.

The second night Paul, the son of Katherine, and CHADD's half-brother, pointed a gun at the head of the bum and told him to leave and never come back or he would blow his head, and CHADD was kicked out in the street in the early morning by Katherine handicapped in his wheelchair.

The Bum began to comfort itself very weirdly until some fake law enforcement in police uniform arrested him. And CHADD was left alone. That is where some fake musician used CHADD until late at night and vanished leaving him in the street, in the cold and the dark sitting in his wheelchair after telling him that a limo would be sent to pick him up, that will come to pick me also, and we will be driven to a five stars hotel all expenses paid. Really!

Instead of a limo, CHADD saw a police car coming to help him, they said. They drove him once again to a mental hospital. CHADD refused all psychotropic drugs. Two hours later a nurse injected him with a drug called aldol. The nurse said that Katherine called the court to get a power of attorney and could bypass the Doctor's orders.

CHADD was admitted to this first hospital the "Memorial Palace" for eight days. At the end of the week, he was told that Katherine, Paul, and his nephew had baked him so he would not be released but sent to another mental facility one hour further for drug reevaluation. CHADD was transported to another mental center for 72 hours completely naked, and like he had been since he was admitted, his Cartier prescription glasses, his Crystal gemstones bids Rosary, and his Gold ring stolen.

Now I understand what it all was about, and I remember clearly Katherine saying "He wanted his freedom and look at what he did with it. "When I heard this phrase I knew she, the archon, was once again part of it. And it was confirmed when she went with him to the first mental hospital he was admitted to to ask for his clothes and his glasses.

I am still fighting these dark energies, the thuggees in medicine, the government that elected itself, the cults, and secret societies including the Freemasons.

That is what happened to CHADD the tainted angel, Baker Acted drugged ward of the state that holds the keys to Divine wisdom to bring humanity into the light of God with me.

This was all orchestrated by the Government with the help of Katherine, Paul, and the nephew hybrids ex-marine. They are part of individuals' dark energy in key places in government, medical systems, school systems, churches, mafia, and secret societies... They are part of the genocide, the reduction of the population to keep controlling humanity in slavery.

It began with the two weird business propositions, followed by the bum, the fake police in uniform, and the second Baker Act of CHADD from the family of Hybrids. They could not admit that two doctors in two previously admitted facilities were setting him free of the Sunshoke illegal program. And it was all orchestrated by the dark forces together in an ultimate gesture to bring him back into drugs to control and manipulate CHADD.

When he was in the first hospital the Memorial Palace, he called Katherine asking her to bring him some clothes. Instead, Katherine asked for and received a power of attorney that allowed her to bypass the doctor's order and inject CHADD without his consent of a drug called Haldol. A combination of aldehyde and alcohol. As this was not enough that is when Katherine, Paul the ex-marine, and a punk nephew, Backer Acted him again.

CHADD was transported an hour away in another county for seventy-two hours. He was released and now he is again the subject of the State.

When they manipulated his brain, before the bum disappeared with the fake police he was given a court order to appear for trespassing that he never physically saw, and he missed his court date of course. He was not aware of it.

He woke up the first morning after his release and was arrested for missing his court date.

"What court did I miss he asked. But no one cared to answer him, and they drove him to jail.

He went to court inside the jail, a parody of justice, and was sentenced to a two thousand bail and back under the guardianship of the hybrid archon Katherine. But she lies to court, and we will see about it. The Light of God is stronger.

So, hearing that I went to sit and pray at the Divine Mercy chapel, opened the Bible, and read "They have not been burned yet, but when they will know who I am"

I called my friend Minister and she said, "I do not see him deprived of his freedom for long" That was confirming my feelings and what I was given to read in the Bible.

Chapter 17

How the Reunion with Eliyana happened

That longtime friend after years without communication between us suddenly reappeared in my life. She was sent to help the God Duo. She spoke.

And it reminds me of when I was so sad just after I left my country and found myself in a third-world country. I had to go to a parking lot on a set day of the week to buy my bread homemade by a German man. He was the only one making fresh bread. Same as buying cheese. Luckily I had the 4 wheels-drive to reach the Italian homemade cheese. Only open Market on Saturday to buy my veggies and fish on the side of the roads. I cried so much for help that a beautiful lady looking exactly like my aunt manifested herself and helped me.

This new event happened on a Friday at about lunchtime. The phone rang and I heard "I am here at the airport. I will stay in your state for a few days. I would like to see you".

Eliyana? Is it you I said

She took me by surprise. I began to remember the beautiful eyes she had and how she was always a joy for her friend to be around.

Great! I said, where are you staying? She replied, in a hotel not too far from you. Then I asked her how she was going to get to her hotel. Have you some kind of transportation, asked. I did not know if someone was waiting for her, and she said "Well, I guess the hotel can pick me up, they must have a transformation" Wait for me Eliyana, I said, I am coming to pick you up."

I was worried wondering if I would recognize her. It has been so long since we saw each other. I arrived at the airport and parked just in front of a woman with an adorable little service dog in her arms and four enormous suitcases plus many small bags.

I stood there staring at the woman until Elyiana broke the staring silence and said "So, you are not going to give me a hug?" At that same time, a man in his thirties grabbed one of the luggage and began to load it in my car. Luckily I was driving a 4WD Atlas.

That is where my navigation system decided to drive all around town to reach her hotel instead of taking the highway. But we finally arrived, and she insisted on taking a quick shower before we could go and have dinner together,

The A/C was not functioning correctly and what I thought would be a quick shower turned out to be ninety minutes and me waiting in my car outside. We finally headed towards a restaurant and did not see the time passing by, I still had to drive back to my house and went to bed at one in the morning. But this was the beginning of a reunion for our missions. Elyiana I was convinced of it, was sent to help the God Duo. And I was right when I finally heard the name of the real Judge of Justice. The one that rules by the Laws of the Constitution.

Chapter 18

Gaby

When I just met my new friend Gaby in a Paris Cafe in September, she struck me as eloquent, thoughtful, and soft-spoken she explained to me:

Taking the sick on a Journey to the other world, a realm of myth and magic to help reclaim sovereignty, destiny, and their authentic self, often lost in the overwhelm of everyday life is what you do and you must continue to do, VIE.

Then I remembered the explanation CHADD gave me on pink noise. Pink noise is the color of noise, not entirely unlike white noise. Both white noise and pink noise contain all the frequencies that are audible to humans — 20 hertz to 20,000 hertz — but the way their signal power is distributed among those frequencies differs. White noise has equal power per hertz throughout all frequencies, while the power per hertz in pink noise decreases as the frequency increases. As a result, the lower frequencies in pink noise are louder and have more power than the higher frequencies. However, most people perceive the sound of pink noise as being even, or flat, because it has equal power per octave. In one study, pink noise increased deep sleep and dramatically improved memory in older adults. "The pink noise enhances brain activity that's associated with deep phases of sleep,

Then I received at 3:33 a very special message from the divine realm that also brought me the energies of love, peace, and prosperity.

And I heard you are receiving a message from the divine realm. You have the full support of your guardian angels.

Chapter 19

Katherine and Paul Join Efforts to Separate CHADD and VIE, and Karma Will Follow

It is Sunday night, I fall asleep for a short time, wake up, fall asleep again, and wake up, over and over. I glanced at the clock and next to it was my cell phone. On my cell screen, it's saying "History is happening. Don't waste any more time, the truth is coming.

In the middle of a long deep dream, I try to breathe slowly, and the scenes continue. Inevitably Karma is coming. How dare they even consider separating the GOD DUO again?

As the God Duo warriors of God sent to Earth by the highest government of the Universe to help this Earth at this time in History, we have difficulty with the violence here. It is so hectic physically, mentally, emotionally. It is a fast-paced roller coaster ride with its ups and downs. With the lack of compassion and love, the hate of CHADD's surrogate Katherine, the half-brother Paul corrupted and Violent, working for the corrupted Government, and the nephew barely in his early twenties lying, stealing, hating, and using girls for sex with no feelings, or any consideration for them.

We are told that it is time for you people to awaken to the reality of who you are, and where you come from. A long and painful task to achieve emotionally and physically for both of us. We do not perceive things the way Earthly does. We are judged and ridiculed for it. We do our best to adjust to your 3D planet and we must live with it.

So, when I reconnected with CHADD eighteen years ago he was in a wheelchair and needed help from psychotropic drugs, hungry, anemic, blind, and in a constant foggy State of mind. It could not even drink or eat on its own. It took me several months to detox him from medications and nourishing him and I could only communicate with him a few moments of clarity each day.

Also, my caring for CHADD was controversial to people who did not approve, and you are going to see why and how eighteen years later we have to be separated, we can't communicate by phone or see each other.

It's around eight o'clock. Like every day Katherine entered CHADD's bedroom with a handful of prescription drugs, and thirteen pills and asked him to open his mouth, gave him a glass of water, and told him to swallow while she looked at him swallowing them. It gives him confusion.

With all the pills that she ingests, she is beginning to lose her memory, sight, and ears and she is diabetic and takes insulin injections every day.

Around Nine o'clock, one hour later, she came back to CHADD with a handful full of the same psychotropic prescription drugs and asked him to take again his drugs.

CHADD told her that she already made him take it at eight. That time, even though every time he confronted her she either Baker Acted him or kicked him out of the house, he defied her and spoke:

"What are you going to say when you are in front of Jesus, and he will ask you why you made me take all these pills?"

Katherine's face changed, she became pale and said, "*I am calling my son Paul and have VIE arrested*".

Paul, her corrupted son, a minute later sent a text to my family.

How did he get the information about where to send the text? One of his previous wives was a private investigator so...

Here is the text Paul sent to my family. Paul is freaking out the court will discover he and Katherine keep CHADD under a roof where all his guns are kept.

"Good morning, Sorry to bother you. I know you've been getting all ends for my mom and everybody else about CHADD and VIE. Sometime this past week I guess VIE came to our town and brought a phone to him that she bought for him because he lost his when he was locked up. They spent the day together and are now talking on the phone again, which teaches them on their own. The problem is that now I overheard VIE guiding me over firearms that are in CHADD on how mom arrested over firearms that are in the house because he's been Baker Act in such those guns were given for my grandfather to my family and with me retired law enforcement. I have mini guns of my own that are stored there as well as at my girlfriend's house, I am putting my foot down now and getting involved in this because I can't keep getting phone calls over things going on with my mom being arrested and threatened by CHADD and coming from VIE, etc. I understand you got your side of things that you must do, and I respect that I'm not trying to be an asshole. My mom is getting older and at this point, I can't have her going through that anymore. This has been years of this. So, I am going to have all the guns removed from the house immediately. I've already installed cameras in an alarm system around the house, and CHADD will be thrown out shortly to come to live with VIE, which is what we were told was going to happen, he will be tossed out of the house very soon. There is no more babying him and getting him help. Things are about to get very bad, and I don't want it to get to the violent side. I must take care of my elderly mother just as you take care of your family. I am not threatening you know the way it's going to have to go from here because I get involved and I don't have time for this shit like anyone else. I would appreciate it. If you could cut VIE off from the conversation with CHADD at all if you can. If you cannot understand just let me know that you tried. I will find ways for it to happen as I am going to spend my vacation trying to make sure this comes to an end. If you have something in store that you feel you could share with me just so that I know or maybe you and I can collaborate on things to try to make this problem disappear. Please let me know as soon as possible as I have to drive tonight and start taking care of this crap and I'm getting very tired of it; the way things are going one or both are going to be locked up and they don't deserve that at all. CHADD is going to be thrown out of the house. Probably anytime now and I have no idea where he's going at this point I don't care. I don't think my mom does either at this point because he was threatening her this morning and it's just enough, please let me know what you could do or are going to do at this point. I am sorry if it's coming across the wrong way. I'm very upset now that my vacation is getting ruined over this again and it's going to come one way or another. Thank you."

Wow! First, I did not bring the phone to CHADD. When was CHADD locked up? Let's talk about it. All his life, Katherine and Paul have him admitted to mental hospitals to make sure that he was kept under drugs and in a foggy state. And every time new drugs came to the market CHADD was forced to ingest it. I found out incidentally Paul was very much involved in the numerous CHADD's Baker Acts and mental hospital admissions. Paul was involved in M-K Ultra. How I found out was when he harassed me on the phone I asked him, why don't you put your daughters into the human experiment project MKUltra? He reacted violently to it.

The thing about the guns is Katherine and Paul are Scared. She lied to the court and swore that there were no guns in her house. As for Paul, not later than three weeks ago he put a gun at the temple of someone CHADD invited into his house and threatened to blow his head off saying, as an ex-law enforcement officer I can easily get away with it.

For the installation of cameras all around the house, it is obvious because they both are not consciously at peace. How could they be, If he is not retired from law enforcement he would have to resign.

Throwing CHADD in the street? That is exactly what they did four weeks ago to send bag him again to send him to a mental hospital for 3 weeks.

Them caring for him? Really? When did they ever care for him? If they had he would not have gotten into a coma due to an overdose of psychotropic drugs. CHADD would not be handicapped by unnecessary surgery and would be walking. He would not have been Baker acted on by them again and again, and to begin with, he would have never been sold to the State since six years old by his family for money purposes.

Stopping Babbying him? Babying him by putting him again and again in mental facilities and kept on drugs? By the baker acting him again and again?

The Truth is Katherine is getting sicker and sicker, she is getting weaker and weaker so now she uses her son Paul to do her dirty job. She does not want CHADD to make it. She knows that he is not of her blood. She knows that I saved him when he was dying mistreated by her and the State while she was living on his money. These shape-shifters with the infiltrated nephew in the Marines have no compassion and are unable to love, lie, twist the truth, and manipulate people.

So, compelled and forced CHADD and I must take a pause. The father takes charge from here, and being his warriors sent to help!

Well, like I said to my family, I forgive them, and I will pray for them. But I don't know if it will make a big difference because once the Father makes his decision, that's it.

CHADD whispered in my ears "God will recall her soon. She went too far. She is refusing to go to the Light. I told you VIE many times that I will not be free until she passes away. But that time she went way too far. And the shape-shifters that they are, her, Paul, and his son hate you."

Yes, They are hating us. CHADD for still being alive and me for being in the middle of her business, like she said.

"All You have to do is to stand up and their little game is over."

And you will see that following this event six weeks later Michael the Archangel will come to CHADD, and I will help.

One day, after being cut from phone communication with CHADD, I received a Phone call. I was about to hang up when I heard his voice saying I was at the Hospital due to an overdose of prescription drugs from the Psychiatrist. But there will not be consequences to it.

Once again Katherine forced it to swallow twice the number of pills he should have. Or she said I will throw you in the street and report to the Court why I kicked you out.

That sad event gave us a chance to speak on the phone, but unfortunately only one time. CHADD was released after a few days. But it did not get better for him. He became trapped in the house. Not only he was under cameras in each room of the house, but he was also not able to get out. The front door once open was now, automatically closing 15 seconds later. Being in his wheelchair and having to turn it at the right angle to take the ramp was impossible to do in fifteen minutes.

That is where Saint Michael met me. He told me a while later ". Between the Mother who received immunity when she sold him to the State, hypnotized everyone who has to do with his life and health, who has authority to speak for him to Social Security, Court, and Hospitals, tell Doctors what to prescribe and what to inject him with, and now get him Psychiatric appointments twice a week for new drugs plus the brother still in contact with some corrupted Law enforcement officers, and the

Nephew that infiltrated the marines, they have too much power. "

He then explained to me that he was split into two. The Protector Michael and the Defender Michael are in power with his sword. That allowed him to do his task as the Defender and as the Protector, and he was going to resolve the problem.

He mentioned "The Dark does not like it when I use my sword. I am going to use it four times. For the three circles, and the other one that does not comply with the constitution but sets up his judgment and rules"

Chapter 20

Will the Coming Ascension Includes Everyone?

I got out of my car when a woman walked towards me and gestured as if she was going to whisper but did not move her lips. I was receiving it by telepathy.

"Hello VIE. The creator has allowed pieces of himself to be broken off, not broken, extended into smaller units to learn of himself. Each piece has been awarded an individual expression that the father is fully aware of. I wish you to understand, there is no separation, but only an illusion of separation. The illusion of separation was found necessary in all experience trials, for when the parts were aware of the whole, they did not seek expression as an individual for they knew they were all." She gave me a big smile and left. I saw her crossing the road and then disappear.

Your soul cannot be satisfied unless doing what you came here to do. Because you came to be of service to humanity and self.

Whenever I give a multidimensional session I am always open to a new experience. It's never twice the same experience.

An interesting thing happened when I gave a healing session to Tania. She was puzzled when she began to hear a voice asking her to deliver this message:

"As the day approaches, the nature of this ascension is becoming increasingly clear. You, all the people, are here on earth today to witness the manifestation of a long-prophesied ascension. This change will be sudden, and the creation of the conditions will manifest heaven on earth.

What many of you do not realize is that you are going to heaven not through physical death, but by the world being risen in the twinkling of an eye. Like.

The earth will rise in vibration because everything physical, body, and the ground beneath your feet, and everything around you will rise in frequency. And you will arrive at the basic realm of heaven, and you will be physical.

It is not for a select few and it is not optional. It will include all of you. Everyone will ascend to a higher physical reality. It is powered by pre-ordained cosmic energies and propelled by Divine agency into a realm of higher natural frequency and higher consciousness. As the day approaches, the nature of this ascension is becoming increasingly clear.

Well! Everyone because all others will have already left the planet"

Chapter 21

Your Ascended Light body

Our civilization is at a crossroads and will be choosing one of two paths during this important window of time. And that choice will have an impact for years to come.

Sitting down in the hotel lobby waiting for my friend to join me, I saw a beautiful woman in her thirties entering. She came with a sweet smell towards me and sat in one of the leather seats next to me. Without looking at me I heard her voice saying: I am pleased to join you today VIE. I am from your spiritual family in another realm, and I bring you a message of hope and love. The time has come to talk about the ascension process.

When you are ascending in body, growing old will not happen. You will continue to look young and vibrant, and it will seem to you that you have arrived in heaven. You will be weightless and will have the sensation of floating. In your early stages of ascension, you will also be able to pass through solid objects and walls.

Most of you who have physical challenges now such as missing limbs or other physical conditions, these illnesses and conditions will disappear when you ascend into your light body. You may have heard this information before, but all need to hear it again for confirmation purposes. It is no longer necessary for any of you to endure these conditions as they are only temporary and are an illusionary world.

CHADD knows he will be walking again.

The appearance of the body will be determined by the vibrational patterns of your light body. These patterns may include everything from a soft glow to an iridescent rainbow. It all depends on your perception as well as what you can hold in your consciousness. In other words, if you have a strong negative or positive perception of yourself, that is what will be reflected. This is another reason to clean up your thoughts to hold pure light and love within your bodies.

Regarding the "aging process," you will continue to grow and expand until you reach your highest potential that is yet contained within the human form. Once you have reached this point, you will cease any further growth.

The original human body is a perfect creation from God. It was not a product of evolution but of intelligent design. It will be your choice whether to upgrade to the new body that awaits all on the New Earth after you ascend.

It will be a fully functioning, complex, and beautiful physical creation far greater than anything you can currently imagine. You will be like gods in your bodies of light, and you will have perfect health, strength, and endurance.

These bodies are physical, not ethereal or ghostly as some have imagined them. They are tangible and solid, although you cannot see them with your eyes as you do the body you now inhabit. These bodies will never age or die. They are indestructible and perfect in every way, even more so than the human form you now inhabit.

The new bodies will be designed to function optimally within the fifth-dimensional environment of the New Earth. The physical world has been transitioning from third to fifth dimensional frequencies of energy for some time now and this process is increasing in speed as we draw closer to the end times.

Because of the higher vibration in which you will live on the New Earth, your bodies must also raise their vibrations if they are to survive there without disintegrating.

When you are in your ascended body, you will not have to worry about growing old. You will continue to look young and vibrant.

The ascended masters get to choose what age they want their bodies to be. They can look like a child or an old man, depending upon what will best help them teach you. They will be with you as well as they too will be in their ascended bodies.

Your children will ascend with you. The light has accelerated your children's growth so that they can come into their bodies of light at the same time as you. They too will look at least 20 years of age when they ascend, but most likely much younger.

Then the woman went toward the front door and simply vanished leaving behind the sweet smell she came in with.

Chapter 22

Francois and a Therapy of Now

All energy is intelligent; it responds to the intentions we hold for it. And can be directed or non-directed; it can be concentrated or scattered; it can be harnessed or dispersed. It all depends on the use to which the intention is put, and it determines the world you experience around. You are the ancestor that changes everything for your bloodline. You are the golden light in human form brought to earth with a higher purpose. You did not come to fear the future but to shape it, and it is foolish to believe that you are insignificant.

Does it make sense to you now? Everyone is gifted but some never open their package.

As the journey continues I am putting the pieces together for you. A month or so later, I received a phone call from my client Tania she said:

"When I walked up the steps leading to a place of DeJa'Vu yesterday it felt so familiar, I experienced something that I never expected."

At that same time, I felt relief. It took all the burden off me, the therapist. I was finally given some feedback. This was proof for me that the world was in progress and changing. Clients were beginning to be in contact with their feelings, and their emotions, and were more aware of their physical bodies. And if you do not believe that people have been programmed then you have been programmed.

This brings me to a session that brought about this new way of thinking, and the way of looking at diseases and the current medicine.

For a couple of years, another client named Francois complained of digestion problems, acid reflux, and pain. Francois had X-rays, Biopsies, and blood tests, and tried various diets with no effects. Then he was diagnosed with a malfunctioning gallbladder by a surgeon and scheduled for surgery. His gallbladder was removed but nothing changed after.

I asked my guides to confirm me, as my intuition was telling me that that was not the problem. And I was right. Francois simply had stones in his gallbladder that could easily be removed. So, I asked a higher source for help. Since Francois never complained again, He has now a new gallbladder the size of a pea, and it functions perfectly. And it is not from a donor. Yes! A new gallbladder grew to replace the one removed. There was a group called in to repair it. This group was assigned to Francois just for that.

Now as I VIE, I radiate the power of God, and God holds the gift of radiating healing energy, and the power of auditory processing into healing energy through a low frequency of 26 Hz. and 91 decibels. That was how my client Tita described me when she discovered the Colour of DNA during her multidimensional healing session.

"VIE I am floating moving into a mist. It feels like my brain is at rest. It is the magnetic field I believe I am experiencing. It is very peaceful. I am standing now on white clouds. I have a loose white robe. Probably made of light and above is a goldish light. It is meeting something going across my forehead and shoulders now. I can feel all, and it is very interesting.

The light is moving from the front of my forehead around to the back of my head. Now the energy is moving to the feet. As I lay down, I saw a couple of Doves. The energy is radiating through the core. To the middle, now radiating my sides. The light is opening the vibrations so I can go into the tube, which is a tunnel. The light is filling the entire tube. It is Gold and I realise it has a life consciousness. I am hearing its purpose is for "immersing, cleansing, blessings, welcoming."

It is pink and blue and lavender and sparkling and green. I feel it is an infusion of knowledge I am receiving. They say it's a necessary step right now from the physical world to the higher realm.

It is a color band, in the DNA. They are layers of misty stuff and there are colours in it. They are bands of color, and each one is a different color. They say that is how it all works.

What scientists can't see is that the DNA is wider and composed of colors. Everything has a code, and the code is equal to a color which gives it its life code. And it's simply the process to be followed.

The color is an energy that is spinning. Colour is part of the formula, but part of the code. It is how the information is transmitted. It creates, and it is all one. It is all shaped into one. It is a color, it is a vibration, a movement, and all at the same time. I see red first. It is the basis. And the next color is so purple it looks black. Then it turns into a beautiful purple and stays. Now it becomes a reddish-orange gold. An unknown color to me. And this one-color move. Each color has a movement in and out of each other. The gold-orange-red moves in continuous motion, and this color has to do with life. It is consciousness, awareness, and knowingness, all of that into one.

Before I even had a chance to bring and address her physical, I was guided to look inside her body, and what needed to be done took place. Looking inside there was a code that needed to be removed because it was not the truth. It was a sensitive code that needed to be removed. It had to be gentle, and because there is a process.

A word about the human clones. Human clones are not original form. It is human and alive, but it is not alive like other people. Because the light is what makes it alive. Because the spirit and the soul come from the source. It comes from Light. Creator God has so much force, it is light, love creation and the other side is just going through the process of the blank. It is blank. It is an empty shell. There is no life expressed from it. You can still create life but in the one created by God, there is a life force but not in the clone.

Chapter 23

Another Dark attack on VIE

I was driving on a sand road, but after taking a wrong turn, I found myself driving on a highway, surrounded by mountains and a lake. It was on a very hot summer day. I arrived in front of a grocery store, with a neon sign making up illegible. As I pulled in for assistance, a large group of tall grey-skinned-looking Asian men with dark glasses poured out of the front door staring at me, and seeming shocked and upset, waving their arms up in my direction. I realized these "tall grey Asian-looking men" didn't even appear to be human, so I drove off.

While driving away, I noticed egg-shaped automobiles were following them. I sped ahead until the weird vehicles were out of sight.

I came back home with a terrible headache. I laid down the time for my headache to pass and went to the pool. Entering the pool, I felt something biting me and did not pay attention to it. That was another horrible physical attack on my body. I was awakened in the middle of the night with the size of a small pea lump in my left breast. I knew it was not cancerous.

I was just meeting Archangel Michael that day and he confirmed it. He asked me to carry sage in my car, in my room, and my purse then told me to put salt at the entrance of my door room, also in a small container behind the door and all along the window. I immediately texted my friend the count from the twelve dimensions and asked him to pray for me as this physical attack was very painful.

Then we drove Michael and me to the Shrine dedicated to Mary the Queen of the Universe. We walked in and went directly to the small chapel located in the back. As soon as I sat down, I was guided to speak the language of the Light. It shifted something in the Church. A woman was standing in the back her hand on her heart in reverence when the Virgin Mary appeared. Then Michael told me, the Virgin Mary was here and said you expelled something inside of you.

I passed the three following days praying for the world and the people in the world in need of prayers. The pain was so intense I could not sleep so I prayed.

Chapter 24

A transfer to a different hemisphere

I woke up one morning with my life suddenly slightly altered. I was driving and I felt a hot sensation within my vehicle, then I heard distant voices, one of which stood out, informing me that I'd been transferred to another place in a different hemisphere.

I heard music coming from my right, turned my head in the direction it was coming from, and saw people wearing what looked to me like 17th-century clothes. The only comprehensible language they spoke was a broken ancient French language.

There was quoting "Let there be Light, and there was light. (Genesis 1:3)"

In the end, dear traveler, on this earthly journey, remember your role as a member of the Family of Light. You are here to guide and unite, to love and heal, and to contribute to the transformation of this beautiful planet we call home.

Embrace the knowledge that the Prime Creator resides within you and all things, and let love be your guiding star. In this grand cosmic dance, as you awaken and elevate, you will play a part in the unfolding of a new chapter for Earth and the universe, where love and unity reign supreme!

Chapter 25

A Sunday Brunch at Michelin's and I am poisoned

I did not sleep well the night before and I was taking a nap when I had the vision of a man that was trying to approach me. I did not like the feeling I was having about that unknown man. He was of an average height and slim. His hair color was not blond but light brown. I was walking on a sideway passing as rapidly as I could the people. Looking from time to time in my back. The man was following me as fast as he could passing the people too trying to catch me. I awoke and the vision stopped.

That Saturday I was meeting a friend for brunch at twelve-thirty at Michelin's restaurant. The traffic on the road was heavy and bumper to bumper. I called Reyna to let her know I would certainly run a little late. But I arrived before her and on time.

The place looked not fancy but amazing with a lot of artists. The restaurant was packed. Luckily Reyna made some reservations for us. Reyna excused herself and went to wash her hands. When she came back the owner with a funny hat came to greet us, wished us a good brunch, and left.

Suddenly I felt someone was trying to pick on my head, then I began to feel sick. I realized I had been poisoned and rushed to the bathroom, but the lady's room was closed and locked. I came back to the table and told Reyna let's pay and leave. The bathrooms are locked, and I do not feel well. Reyna looked at me and said: It is funny when I went to wash my hands earlier it was also locked. I had to go to the men's bathroom, but this was much earlier.

I reached into my purse and found three activated charcoal and swallowed two of them. It took about 20 minutes to take effect. We left for a place with all kinds of freshly brewed organic tea.

This event took place after the end of days of pain by an attack on my left breast. Just two days after my breast was ill.

One week later in the middle of the night, my body began to release a strong odor. I understood I needed a good detox from these non-stop attacks. The water was so dark that I could not see my feet and the coil was smelling. Which I never had before.

Chapter 26

I am asked to share a message of great importance

I was enjoying a good cup of coffee listening to music with my eyes closed, observing my breathing, and paying attention to any sensations in my body. Epiphany or striking insights bestowed by the divine. It came to me when I least expected it.

"This message is of great importance, and we must share it with you. There are only a few humans that have received your knowledge because you have been the chosen one.

At that moment in time, some are in fear of the unknown and others are thirsty for the truth and can't find it or just a little bit here and there.

It is like Anne-Sophie, the woman who contacted you the other day, she is a perfect example. She wants to Know more. She told you, she read seventy percent of the world's population must be reduced and the oligarchs must be stopped. But how and who are they, she asked you.

So, here it is. What is happening is very complicated for them to understand. It is time they heard it. The planet is in World War III. It is the last battle between good and evil. Where extraterrestrial beings are involved in it.

The seven Trumpets were celebrated a few days ago. The White hats are involved too. It is spiritual, political, and global. A group that goes back to Roman times and has controlled the populations since then is in this battle. The Perfecti Knight Templars are back on earth. Like the Indian Thugees, Ascended Masters, Archangels, and Saints are back to help. All members of the Cabal and their minions must be taken out of the planet and of the power they have elected themselves in. While the military takes control.

GESARA/NESARA (a fixed number of thousands of US dollars) will be given to all citizens. One hundred and twenty days after new elections for new governments will take place.

The good thing is that all illegals have to go back to their original country of birth when GEASRA/NESARA will apply.

This happens at the same time the new Earth shifts its vibration. The Schumann resonance is changed, and the Fifth dimension replaces 3D. There is the split of the planet Earth in two, and the return of Jesus and Mary Magdalene in Oneness soon to come.

I know that you are waiting for YHWH and He will come back like a thief in the night, he said, with his wife soon. And what they did not want you to know, He was married to Mary Magdalene.

But be aware, prepared, and ready to see it through when the Cabal will try to project a holographic scene of an Aliens invasion and a fake prophet with fake Angels and Saints."

Chapter 27

Traveling through a Portal to Enlightenment

A stargate is a portal to other worlds, realms, and dimensions. It was on a late Sunday night. I finished my cup of tea, fell asleep, and left my body for another adventure.

I embarked on a journey into the enigmatic realm of 0010110, when the boundaries of time and space blend, and the power of telepathic connections becomes reality. Another dimension that is not a different place, is another lifetime.

Be prepared to be immersed in a world of boundless potential, where the human spirit units to shape realities yet imagined.

Join us as we explore the awe-inspiring trillion-year mission to craft the universe of awakening. Delve into the concept of parallel timelines, when the past, present, and future intersect. Witness the creation of an immortal code to the shared consciousness of humanity's spirit.

So, after the ambassador from the 12th dimension contacted me, a Count from the 12th contacted me, Padre Pio, Saint Maria Faustina Kowalska, Saint Sarah, and more came to help us CHADD and VIE with our mission, Saint Michael joined to battle, and Mother Mary appeared to us in the Shrine dedicated to her. The Queen of the Universe. The king of the Universe is coming back soon.

Chapter 28

I Entered a Portal While Meditating

Today I entered and traveled a stargate to another world, a portal while meditating. Meditation is the stairway to Heaven, resurrection, and enlightenment. Meditation is the portal to enlightenment and now I can share.

The Ascension is a descent into the heart. It is not about getting somewhere or reaching Someplace else. It is about acquiring a vision that allows us to see what has always been there.

I was lying down in bed, frozen by a suspicious noise. I said a prayer and took a breath. I was not there in my room but in my thoughts. I took another breath, then I thought what do I do now? Then I heard a voice that came from silence. I am not sure what I was expecting. And I got a clear message written "Wings surround your body, and your hands are pressed to your heart with a gaze directed to the father upward. Your hands are pressed in prayer. In a region in France, known as Camargue, there is a cross that is associated with Mary Magdalene. It is called La Croix de Camargue. It is also known as the Guardians Cross. It represents faith, the anchor of the local fisherman at the bottom represents hope and the heart in the middle represents the love of the three Marys who arrived in the Camargue in the wake of Christ."

Saintes-Maries-de-la-Mer has a church with a crypt for Saint Sarah known to the Romani (the Gypsy) people as the Queen of the outsiders. Saint Sarah (pronounced by the Gypsy San Sarah) had a vision that Mary Magdalene present at Christ's crucifixion would arrive on their shores. When the three Marys, Mary Magdalene, Mary, and Mary Salome, arrived on a ship without sails to Saintes-Maries-de-la-Mer, Saint Sarah was the first to welcome them with open arms. Mary Magdalene lived thirty years North of Saintes-Mary-de-la-Mer in a cave (grotte) at la Sainte Beaume, the Holy Cave. Mary Magdalene's gospels reveal she was a leader among other leaders. She could turn the disciples back toward God; non-radical an apostle to the apostles; non-radical and heretical than a prostitute.

The Gospel of Mary Magdalene wasn't among the Nag Hammadi findings of the Dead Sea Scrolls. But, the Nag Hammadi, and these discoveries, Help us contextualize Mary's Gospel and understand why all these scriptures were considered dangerous enough to want to destroy it.

The similarity between the Gospels found in the Nag Hammadi library and the gospel of Mary Magdalene, the common theological thread, all emphasize the importance of remembering Christ within the appearance of Mary Magdalene holding an alabaster jar filled with the Holy Oil to anoint Jesus Christ before burial is significant to place her in the tradition of Priest and Priestesses of Isis. Whose unguents were to achieve the transition on the threshold of death while retaining consciousness.

The Contemplative prayer, the Byzantine mystics known as Hesychasts practice originate as early as the fourth century in the Eastern Orthodox Church.

Chapter 29

Shifting a Stagnant Energy

The Holy Spirit made me shift the stagnant energy for the entire planet. It is a field that works through all times and realms. I traveled to the portal and met my star sister. She guided me to the Cathedral "Notre Dame de Paris". I saw that the floor plan of the Cathedral is the relationship between the alchemical oblong square and the electrical circuit of the brain. Oblong square is three enveloping circles with the center circle square, she said. Then we traveled to other European Cathedrals, and I saw the same.

Then we moved to travel to the Vatican City and I was a witness to be given to see that when the energies of the third eye located between the two pillars of the cerebral hemispheres are in equilibrium, you resonate as a harmonic waveform generator. It was right there on the ceiling for me to see.

It was followed by a visit to the Vatican Library. Miles of books. I was wondering what was next for me to learn, One book fell off one shelf. I opened it and read: Life is the union of masculine and feminine converts energy creating a divine spark within an oblong square of capsule. A cosmic egg that manifests itself as a soul.

I picked the next book on the shelf and here is what I found:

> A+U+M pronounced Om is associated with a mystical spiritual tool. A+U+M corresponds to the three stages of cosmic creation. Before the sixteenth century the letter U was not written and used. It was transcribed as V in Latin and AUM was written AVM about the Latin Ave Virgo Maria. Hail Mary the Virgin. It is used by Catholics when they are practicing meditative prayer, praying the Rosary. Also called "Le Chapelet" AVM or AUM is used as a mantra.

You do not have to be a Catholic to use this meditative prayer. It only takes about 20 minutes to pray the rosary. This powerful prayer allows you to meditate on Scripture and the key moments during Jesus' life.

The Rosary defining moment came during an apparition to Saint Dominic around the year 1221. Saint Dominic was combating a popular heresy in France called Albigensian, Mary gave him the Rosary, told him to teach people this devotion, and promised that his apostolic efforts would be blessed with much success if he did. It is known that the order Saint Dominic founded (the Dominicans) played a major role in promoting the rosary throughout the world in the early years of this devotion.

Here is how to pray the rosary is quite easy and powerful: While you are holding the crucifix make the sign of the Cross. With your hand tough your front and say: in the name of the Father, the middle of the chest the Son, the Left shoulder the Holy Spirit, On the Right shoulder Amen.

Say one Our Father... three Hail Marys...one Glory be..., then on the next large bid Our Father... on each small bead of the decade, pray the Hail Mary...

Chapter 30

The Ethereal and Intangible Realm, and Spirituality

This is an invitation for you to hold the empowered to be a co-play on the planet. For that, you must know and understand some hidden or withheld information from you.

The process here is designed to connect you even deeper. The transition from 3D to 5D life will open a higher state of being. 3D is characterized by separation while the 5th dimension vibrates at a frequency of Love.

Unity and self-expression with the proper preparations and by releasing density emotions, fear, and traumas, your cells will become crystalline conduits for 5D frequencies. You will then ride effortlessly the Ascension wave into an exalted state of harmony, peace, and enlightenment. You will realize your innate connection with all life and revere the planet as a conscious living being. With less limitation and access to your higher self.

You may develop telepathic abilities, intuition, psychic awareness, and new forms of communication. You will likely communicate directly through your heart.

In the fifth dimension, the veil of illusion will be lifted that was imposed by the matrix. Your focus will turn away from materialism and external power, shifting inward. You will see how you create your reality and the responsibility for your part of co-creation. Creating a peaceful world.

Now, spirituality does not come from religion, but it comes from the Soul. There must not be confusion between religion and spirituality. While religion is a set of rules, regulations, and rituals created by humans, which were supposed to help people spiritually. Due to human imperfection religion has become corrupt, politically divisive, and a tool for power to struggle. Spirituality is not theology or ideology. It is simply a way of life., pure and original as given by the highest. Spirituality is a network linking humans to the highest. Father God.

The souls always remain intact. Despite what you have heard, with the "expression selling your Soul". Your Soul cannot be broken or sold. Selling your Soul means that you know you did something that is going to hold your Soul's evolution back, such as selling out for power, fame, or material possessions. By selling your Soul you likely have to amends, repeat the life lesson, or take on a negative karma that you will eventually have to repay.

You did not come here to chase money, obsess about fame and power, indulge in meaningless pleasure, or destroy your body with poison. You came here to remember your true self as incarnate spirit, and to make a difference on this planet.

The Biblical Armageddon prophesied to occur for centuries has been canceled. Thanks to the planet that learned its lessons and passed the test, almost all on Earth will go through graduation and will experience Ascension. Instead of spontaneous Light body activation, we get to keep our physical bodies. It will be graduation into a human life where ordinary people will quickly begin getting incredible abilities.

Even though your physical brain is in 3D, your mind spends much time in the 4D Conscious Level.

Chapter 31

A Thought Ball is Thrown at VIE and CHADD Gets Helped

It happened I was browsing at the big farmers market full of exotic and natural products when a woman approached me. In a very weird accent, she told me her name was Sonia, and in a nearly inaudible voice said, "I was waiting for you" She looked like coming from another time, or world if you prefer. I was wondering if it was real or if I was having a vision. But Sonia continued.

"Each step on a journey is different; chaos is a temporary phase between one natural state of harmony and its transformation into a higher form. Today, we are in the storm before the calm. Chaos is a temporary phase between one natural state of harmony and its transformation into a higher form.

The transition phase between the two states becomes very rough until the higher form is reached. Humanity must awaken now. With the holographic movie projection world people are trapped in the matrix, and many people are dying.

As you know CHADD decided to come to this world and take the pain of others. But he never thought it would be so ugly and it would turn out to this extent to his body. His body has been much more damaged than you think. He is being sent to help with the regeneration of his body and what is necessary to fight disease, because he has more work to do.

And you VIE, you have today wounded behind your ear and in three places in your back from the time when you were stabbed to death once. It's psychic scars coming back. You see it is another thing that no one knows. One of the designs that was put in the COVID is to connect with the past of the souls. This Covid-19 is linked to the past. When you died you were stabbed in the back and under your ears.

Then lately you had stomach problems. You were attacked by invisible dark forces. A thought ball was thrown at you. They have put a harsh intent in a circle and thrown it infecting your solar plexus and your knees. They do not want you to succeed and be rewarded for your work. They tried to weaken and discomfort your body. They force open the sphincter valve in your body that does not lose, and the valve lets it all get back up in the throat.

Chapter 32

A Deliberate Destruction of Knowledge

God told me "You have a mouth use it" At the time everyone was covering it with a mask. Today I must use the knowledge I received to let you all benefit from it. The secret of the true prayer is to forget the things you think you need. In prayer, you overlook your specific needs as you see them and let go into God's hands. Illness was made by your mind at a larger level. Be Prepared for the great Awakening is about to take place.

Today the responsibility lies within you to uncover the best you can. Knowledge was kept from humanity purposely hidden or by accident. Yet still, certain information was merged with cultural traditions and is now regarded as a myth.

Be prepared with my word and your trust in me. Saith God. What you are about to see will shake people to their core. It will be shocking to see what people never thought they would see or what they thought could never take place.

My children this is not to bring fear these warnings are for you to have your heart fixed on me. So, fear does not come in and torment or lead you in the opposite direction. In this time, you are living in things that will be moving.

There are tons of people removed from their position of power or they are stepping down and supposedly retiring. They are removed and not by choice.

God is going to remove people who do not belong there. He is going to expose every single person that is opposed to his plan. And justice is going to be served. You will see court cases overturned. You will see others thrown out. You will see the highest court make decisions you never thought they would. They are about to do their job without turning away and rejecting those cases. It is now time for the highest court to uphold and the one who objects will be removed by me, saith the Lord.

So, God is going to throw out cases and decisions of some judges that were not justifiable.
When a thief has been caught he has to give it back sevenfold: Proverb 6:31. Because God is the judge over all judges.

Chapter 33

One of VIE Weird Encounters

It was mid-afternoon on a Wednesday. I was backing up my car in the driveway when the phone rang. I heard a man with a Pakistani accent:

"VIE do you remember me. My aunt introduced you to me. You said that I had my hair too long. I have cut it. I cut it 10 inches shorter".

And before I could say anything, not even hello, he hung up. What was that about? From a Thuggee! That was the second time I had this type of brief phone call.

About five years ago I received a phone call while I was walking my dog.

"VIE, please tell me that I am not insane. The trees are talking to me." I laughed and reassured him. I told him the story of the eighteen-year-old girl who came to my booth during a convention to experience my energy session. At the end of the session, she was astonished. She was able to hear the radio loud and clear. So, he was not insane. But to continue what he was doing, he hung up. I never knew who he was or how he knew my name. Never heard from him again.

The other was a woman who asked to see me in the office. She came and was barefoot. She explained she had no idea how she came here from Brazil. She went on to say that growing up she loved to escape from her parent's surveillance to run barefoot in the woods. She would enjoy talking to the animals and enjoyed her conversation with the birds. Then she left the office.

Around midnight my phone rang. A man was telling me that he took some marijuana and now has terrible anxiety. He was baptized and became Christian but never practiced, he said. Then still with me on the phone said, now I am walking outside the building to breathe. Then he hung up to call me again at 2 am to tell me the same story. I gently told him he awakened me and to call me in the morning. I never heard from him again.

As I said we are at a crossroads. All these people are searching for reconnection with God. And they don't know it because the actual society is led by Satan.

Chapter 34

Navigating the Hyper Novelty Effect

I asked the inevitable question ...He had an interesting healing, even though he thought was difficult!

When Ivan came into the scene He was standing, but not on the ground. He was standing in a bubble. It was holding him easily but felt like a blown-up surface, so it had a certain tension. Like some stretched material.

I feel like floating in space somewhere. I feel like I am an observer looking down. I am waiting for something to happen.

Another being just popped up. It just appeared in front of me. Like it is going to take me somewhere or be somewhere with me.

The bottom of the bubble opens up, it's like a slide to another part of the universe. I am in the sky floating with CHADD.

Now in CHADD, I view it as transmuting into an understanding of what it is about evolving.

It is about understanding the higher purpose of it all, evolving back to the source. Showing beings evolving back to the source with Divine healing and Reconnection to the disconnected heart. Gaining enlightenment. Helping to shift thereafter to 5D. And Ivan is the perfect example.

He was supposed to gain enlightenment through the experience. But it served and allowed others to understand.

And CHADD and I are your messengers. We are bringing you the explanation for your uncomprehensive anxiety and anguish and the solution to it.

Anxiety human beings are experiencing, and do not understand. They do not understand why, it is the Universe about exhausting paranoia, anguish, and anxiety.

It is emotions of anxiety before breakthrough because you cannot achieve it intellectually. It is coming from nowhere. You cannot comprehend it and you do not know how to overcome it.

It feels like a gate to hell, but you must go there. You must let go of the 3D thinking.

You must drop your third-dimensional thinking. Drop and go away from your name, your identity, who you are, and your title. Also, from who they are and begin to use and rely on your intuition, use discernment.

You are beginning to expand your consciousness. You are coming to the light. You are beginning to awaken, and you are confronted with another reality. Not the fake the cabal have kept you under with their lies. You were kept for a long time in a holographic reality projection and a program. And now you are beginning to understand the covid, Parkinson's disease, the implanted disease. You are waking up slowly. Questioning.

You are losing footing stability. What you thought was is taken away from you, in a universe you have never been before, and still finding your way.

It is humanity versus the control system you live in. Humans are in a difficult situation right now as you are on your way to being enlightened. You are in a dark place with anxiety.

You are becoming enlightened through the process. For some a foot in 3D and one foot in 5D. The old way is dying, and it is painful and hard work. And for some of you, it is the reason you have or are isolating yourself. You are confronted at the same time with other souls on earth that are not awakened yet, and you cannot communicate anymore at the same level. You are opening up your mind.

You are overwhelmed when you realize things like the F.E.D. is not federal but just Bankers' gangsters. You come to hear new things you never heard of before like the Blue Hats are the United Nations Army. Serving the NWO and the invasion of the borders. When you come to have more clarity of mind like governments arrest and put you in jail if you are caught trafficking or using drugs. But they are the first to use these substances and get money from it. And with your discovery that led you to anxiety you are lowering your frequency, and subject to dark and negative energy attacks.

And the solution to healing from these panic attacks and anxiety has nothing to do with psychotherapy, and you understand it also. Because the cabal are the ones that created this degree. They knew at one point you would begin to question your reality and beliefs.

Unfortunately, it is like drugs. It will be a Band-Aid. The cabal has disconnected you and will be able to keep you in a loop in its holographic movie projection.

You came here to Earth at that specific time to help. These Illuminati in power for years do not want to lose the control they have had over you for so long. You are their slaves and money-makers. and they use their negative and invisible forces to attack you in many ways. Adding to your anxiety attack.

All that was to be looked up and brought to your attention so you would remain strong and make it. Until you understand it all and align with your higher purpose.

Understand that Jesus' name is a powerful weapon. The name of Jesus is your supernatural protection, your emergency number, and your rescue number. It responds immediately.

All and everything are spirits, and the anxiety is also a spirit, and it attacks. Just say 'I rebuke you in the name of Jesus Christ of Nazareth." Or "You have no power over me, in Jesus Christ of Nazareth's name." It is important to say Jesus Christ of Nazareth because other humans named Jesus.

Chapter 35

Exciting NEW and TIME

As I draw the cosmic curtains on this exploration, it's been quite a ride of discovering and events. Just imagine my frustration.

While CHADD is kept by the judge in the court order, the corrupted Psychiatrist, and by the surrogate archon Katherine he is kept in her house and forced to ingest thirteen drugs a day. She continues to come with this number of poisoning drugs in her hand and force it into his mouth. "Swallow these or get out of my house. I don't care if you live in the street. Your monthly government check comes directly to my bank account" She told him. And life continues to unfold without him. He is trapped without a life or any friends.

But beware of the Almighty Katherine, he is my blue flame, and I am on my father's mission to reconnect souls.

When you as a conscious disciple manage the Violet Flame, a parallel activity of the Violet Flame is initiated internally. This results in the vibrational awakening of your chakras. Therefore, each time you use the gift of the Violet Flame you are asked not only to focus your attention on what you want to transmute but also on the internal activity which takes place within yourself.

One of the consequences of the continual use of the Violet Flame is the accelerated awakening of all your chakras, you will, step by step, wake up in a different world from where you live now.

Higher consciousness adds more abilities to the ones we have already developed. Intuitive perception leading to perfect synchronicity is a perfect example of the growth that awaits us as we step into the New Reality.

Now the perception of experiential time varies with the frequency of consciousness. Experiential time runs faster at higher frequencies. The shift from Old Reality consciousness to New Reality, heart-centered consciousness includes a shift in our perception of time.

The key to understanding this is that life in the objective world is a projection of the greater reality that exists within you. As people's frequency of awareness rises through fourth-density consciousness, they will become more attuned to the synchronicity that is offered by an experiential approach to time. The more people become mentally attuned to others, the more they manifest synchronicity in their lives.

Sound and vibrations play a key role in our history. Imagine what different kinds of frequencies can do to our bodies which are 70% made of water. Shortly, future medicine will be resonance, vibrational-based, not chemical-based.

The origins of different eye colors can often be traced to specific star systems or ET races. For example, bright blue is linked to the Pleiadian star system, green to Orion, while shades of purple and violet may indicate a connection to Sirius or Andromeda. The Lyrans are associated with turquoise eyes.

Rarer eye colors represent ancient galactic DNA and soul memories carried over from past incarnations on other planets. The distinct blue, silver, purple, or turquoise hues reflect the advanced extraterrestrial genetics and higher frequency energies these souls carry within their auras.

Shifting or changeable eye color can signify a Star seed's ability to tune into different vibrations and dimensions. Their eyes are like portals that provide a glimpse into the many lifetimes their eternal essence has experienced across the multiverse. Their distinctive eye color is a reminder of their cosmic origins and infinite spiritual journey through consciousness.

Remember? I told you while CHADD was put in one of the many psychiatric hospitals, he had a thuggee female doctor able to change her eye color. She changed it but had no soul. She was a reptilian hybrid.

Delving into this fascinating realm might unveil more about your celestial roots and provide insights into the cosmic journey you're on. Many Star seeds feel a telepathic connection with higher dimensional beings, receiving guidance, messages, and healing from these allies. From the Pleiades to Venus, our diverse origins unite us for a cosmic mission.

Chapter 36

VIE New Mission

I have been receiving a great deal of information about the coming shift. Much of it has already been written in my previous books. And yet the information continues to come.

As each great disaster brings Earth closer to a shift, Michael contacted me again to let me know the Father had added me to a new mission. And I received my new assignment. I will have to add to my Reconnective healing session the Divine Reconnection to help people make the transition into the next dimension.

Some will resist because of fear and misunderstanding and just apprehension, and I won't force it because of free will. Free will is respected universally. I just have to persuade individuals, because it is for their good to evolve.

Those who raise their vibration will ascend into the New Earth as it evolves and is lifted into a different dimension. Thus, becoming invisible to the ones left behind.

The Earth is going through horrible times, and there will be an overlay. There will be two Earths, one will overlay the other. Some will choose to remain on the Earth and will be having negative experiences, and others may choose to be on the new Earth. The thing is they won't be aware of each other. They will experience the shifting into the new vibration. That will be a whole new thing if the entire universe shifts at one time.

It will be experienced as beautiful waves of energy. That energy will flow out into the universe. It will be beautiful. But the ones on the old Earth will not know this is happening.

Clair was one of the first sent to me for reconnection. The new Clair had to be confident enough when she awakened. So, at the beginning, most of what she saw was a smoke screen, then little snippets of information in her mind. Because her mind would never be able to handle it all. The problem is not the brain, it is the mind. There are no concepts within the human mind to allow us to comprehend all the complexities of it.

But she had gone through major lifestyle changes with her sister's death. She was ready to awaken and expand her mind to encompass new ideas and theories but in small morsels.

What I am given shows that human minds are awakening. This is the only way human beings can handle the concept of Earth changing frequency and vibration to shift into a different dimension.

Humans had to come to Earth and go back to the 3rd dimension to learn more, to advance spiritually back to the 4th and the 5th and the 6th dimensions.

On Earth, you lose who you are. You lose all your memories of who you are. You don't know that you have a light body. And everybody's so lost. It is not easy. Earth is dense.

We could get all of our energy from the light. The Universe is full of light, the Universe is all light, And it is only in a three-dimensional body that you can get enough light so you can live. You always live, always. Light body can be put to sleep, but generally always live. Negative energy is not light, chaotic energy, disruptive, and very powerful.

Their violence against Christians continues to run rampant in some parts of the world including killings, sexual abuse, and the destruction of homes and churches

But as more people wake up to their divine nature and innate spiritual powers, it liberates strong currents of light, love, and unity consciousness.

This dramatic shift in the collective human energy field causes a domino effect, stirring these higher dimensional realms.

Chapter 37

CHADD and VIE, and The Changing World

It was during Wintertime. I was seated in the living room. I suddenly felt myself shifting, kind of splitting. Being human, and becoming an energy, just a spirit, though in a human form. The feeling was weird.

Then I found myself looking at a strangely familiar place, although it did not resemble any place on Earth. I identify it as that feels like home. It is a good feeling. The buildings are all pink spires. I am way above the planet, and all I can see are different sizes of spires like gigantic crystals, but they are buildings shining and looking crystalline. Now what I see looks like small modern houses of each of a different color. Interestingly, the color depends on the person's energy that lives in it.

I feel I am here and there at the same time. I have not been back there for a while. I came to Earth to get information. I see that the planet is expanding.

I was chosen to be the door to the Divine. I did not decide, I have been chosen. I am here to do energy work to heal and reconnect people to the source and who they are.

To heal someone, you must have the highest pure intention. I connect to the source, and then I can direct it to wherever it is needed.

Catholicism is not a religion. Catholicism is a Christian tradition and a community. It is comprised of faith in Jesus Christ, theologies, and doctrines characterized by specific liturgical ethical, and spiritual orientations and behavior. Unfortunately, since the Roman time Catholicism has been attacked and infiltrated by dark energies to push away parishioners from their faith. Specifically, now with the Vatican and the Pope's recent approval of same-sex marriage.

The word Catholic is derived from the Greek *Katholikos* meaning *universal,* and from *Kath'holou* meaning on the *whole.* You do not have to pray or read the Bible in a certain language. Catholicism is universal and for all.

Jewish religion is a Judaism, monotheistic religion. It is an ethnoreligious group, meaning that they are both an ethnicity, a group identified by common group identity and, usually, language and ancestry, and a religion. You must read and pray the Torah in Hebrew language, in Aramaic. The Jewish religion is only for Jews.

Islam is a Muslim religion, historically called Mohammedanism. Followers of Islam are called Muslims. Muslims are monotheistic and worship Allah. You must pray the Quran in Arabic. Quranic Arabic is the form of Arabic in which the Quran (the holy book of Islam) is written. Islam is only for Muslim people.

The world is moving forward. The world is changing. We CHADD and I are God's warriors; we are witnessing the true color being revealed to the public from above.

Earth and humanity are under construction while business is still open. The DS is in full panic mode, desperate and wounded, and is lunging wild attacks. Satanic energies cannot be hidden anymore as it is prevalent for all to see throughout the matrix society. Nazi Israel Jews created Hamas.

Central banks are shutting down, bankrupt. Old systems went bankrupt, and Congress, the white house, the IRS, the Feds, Federal Reserve were shut down. U.S. Corporation is bankrupted.

Gold-backed currency, digital assets, QFS, Nesara Gesara is Growing!

QFS Nesra Gesara is manifested. The Global/Galactic Alliance is still working on removing the vise-grip on humanity from the DS cabal, currency removing the satanic spell on the global mass.

The political elites in control tell the average people there is an existential crisis with so-called climate change. So much so that climate change alarmism is probably the greatest cause of mental health crises in the world. But the solutions they give to climate change are far worse and more harmful, costing human lives, especially in Europe during the time that heating is needed.

You have been lied to and conned by the rich globalist money-hungry elites. You could have been driving water-powered cars today that release zero pollution. It looks like the Great Awakening journey will be more intense and get more turbulent.

As human consciousness rises, and the control system dissipates, we will see the re-emergence of great technologies. Light will come when humanity enters a higher state of consciousness and enlightenment is a time when there is no more suffering, greed, poverty, war, or negativity on Earth. Humanity will live in peace and prosperity in alignment with the divine purpose for all. It is a time when there is no more suffering, greed, poverty, war, or negativity on Earth. Humanity will live in peace and prosperity in alignment with the divine purpose for all.

Chapter 38

Activation of Consciousness

The Spirit woke me up at 3:30 am this morning, telling me to deliver this message to you. The Universe is always giving you an opportunity, but you have to take it!

"When the Photon Belt's light beam contacts the pineal gland, we will become completely conscious. The pineal gland has been referred to as the "third eye" or "inner eye." It was believed by Ancient traditions it was the seat of enlightenment and could open the mind to higher states of consciousness.

With the activation of your full consciousness and all your 12 strands of DNA, you will gain the ability to manifest and create with your thoughts and intentions. It is an incredible power that allows you to generate anything you need or desire through focused thought and intention. Survival will be easy.

You will warm yourself and adjust the temperature in your environment just by thinking about it. There will be no need for heaters, blankets, or fires. You will be able to Light up a dark space just by intending and focusing your thoughts on the area. You won't need lamps, candles, or electricity. You will Manifest your food, water, and other resources simply by consciously creating it with your mind. Survival will be easy. You will transport yourself instantly to any location you think of. Your enhanced consciousness gives you full access to teleportation abilities. No more diseases, drugs to ingest, no need to seek an M.D. You will heal your body and restore health just by directing your thoughts and energy. You'll be able to self-heal any illness or injury.

You won't need phones or devices; you will communicate telepathically with others who have activated consciousness.

The possibilities are endless. Anything you can conceive of and intend can be manifested directly from the unlimited creative power of your consciousness. Just by thinking about it, you make it. The activated higher consciousness within you opens a world of limitless potential! Your thoughts and intentions become creative forces capable of shaping and manifesting your reality.

With practice and focus, you can master the art of creation and manifestation with your mind alone.

The impending arrival of the Photon Belt will usher in a new era of enlightenment for humanity. This forthcoming shift in human consciousness will mark a significant milestone in human evolution.

Rather than reacting with fear approach this transition with openness. The days of darkness will symbolize a time for rest, reflection, and preparation. The activation of the Pineal Gland can represent new awakenings, and the awakening of latent abilities reminds humanities of untapped potential.

Rather than anxiety meet the future with curiosity and hope. The coming months may prove challenging, but humanity has weathered storms before and emerged stronger. Cling to love, maintain positive visions, and support each other, and you can navigate any darkness into the dawn of a new day.

The promise of DNA activation and increased brain usage reveals possibilities for creation and manifestation humans can barely imagine."

Chapter 39

CHADD and VIE Preparing the Followers Path

I am bringing that forth from a higher source. I am bringing the healing energy from this very powerful information. There is information attached to the words.

It's for human higher goods, for their higher understanding, and their evolution.

I see myself through different stages. It feels like different stations, or different posts, or getting different information. I feel Like I am not in a physical form at that moment. I feel confined and also very free. I know it's to help other people.

I remember being on a planet with a much higher vibration. My allergies are me fighting to be away from this planet, from the energy here on planet Earth. By constantly blocking the lower vibrations. I was chosen to come at this time, the door to the divine. What an honor!

I know coming at this time would be painful. Here is the reason for doing that. It is to bring knowledge to help people in the future. It's about teaching. CHADD who came with me, to prepare the path for those who follow him has a problem adjusting to these, forced to ingest drugs. The daily thirteen prescription psychotropic pills disable the ability to make conscious decisions.

So, none of these people knew before we did Re-Connection on them. They are now allowed to have the information because it is time to acknowledge who they are and their purpose on Earth at this time. There are too many in the wrong direction not working together.

There are many Earth changes coming. Now it is time to call for the subconscious to get some answers that man was unable to access. Some pieces are being lost that have to be passed. The concern is the changes mankind is bringing. Lies are the real danger.

Mankind as a whole is wiping out the knowledge of the balance; the ability to balance between nature and himself. It is a very destructive power and energy. CHADD is here to set up with me a new way of living, a new way of being born, a new way of existing between lifetimes, and a new way of dying so that the cycle of pain is not started. To create new experiences, when people become more conscious of who they are, of their divine nature, less focused on the pain and suffering, and the shame.

More aware of their reasons for living; less intoxicated with those ideas that learning must come through pain. Those intoxicated with those ideas can become aware and conscious of the ideas that one can live and grow and learn through joy, peace, and love.

Chapter 40

Archangel Michael Message

"The Earth will never go back to the way it used to be. The Earth vibration is collecting all the light from the human healers and dispersing it through the Universe, filling the dark cracks that evil entities have left on this Earth for thousands of years.

Humanity, he says, please connect with your pure light of soul daily. Humans must band together, to join as a group and become one Light, One Love. The heartbeat of the Universe is giving you Light codes to upgrade to defend and protect one's soul, to give you intuitive wisdom on the journey ahead.

There are times when you may need to use your armor and battle. Stand strong in the Light of the world and be a beacon for others who cannot see. I will stand beside you and giving you assistance as needed.

You are not alone; the angels are also stepping forth ready to help you."

Many people in society today feel pressure to conform to an immediate social group.

Though making choices, and experiencing the results of those choices, is what human life is all about.

Inner alignment means becoming more of your true self. Your inner being is your true self, and by developing your inner potential, you express more and more of your true self.

When a person manifests their own unique, inner being, they become aligned. When many people in society become aligned in their power, the whole becomes far more influential than the sum of the parts. It becomes exponentially more powerful.

Do not let anxiousness or frustration take over. Reclaim your identity. Trust your higher wisdom. Look to the grander vision.

Chapter 41

Cosmic Genome and Dormant DNA

Star seeds sometimes referred to as lightworkers, Earth angels, or volunteers, star seeds intuitively know they are here to serve a greater purpose.

Although star seeds appear in humans, their souls are imprinted with sacred geometries, celestial energies, and cosmic memories that reflect their home worlds. Many feel a heart connection to specific star systems like the Pleiades, Sirius, Lyra, Andromeda, Orion, and Arcturus.

Star seeds have an innate sense of not fully belonging that stems from carrying the vibrations, light codes, and blueprints of their celestial origins within their DNA. They share a collective galactic and multidimensional lineage across space and time. Star seeds carry dormant DNA from distant star systems within their human blueprint. Although these cosmic genomes lay hidden, star seeds feel an innate calling to reconnect with their higher extraterrestrial abilities and galactic origins.

Although star seeds appear human, their souls are imprinted with sacred geometries, celestial energies, and cosmic memories that reflect their home worlds.

Many feel a heart connection to specific star systems like the Pleiades, Sirius, Lyra, Andromeda, Orion, and Arcturus.

Chapter 42

Digital Life and Stargates

Once again I left my body and lost track of time and traveled to another dimension. Not that I wanted to but... I felt a deep vibration. Knowledge is a blessing, not a curse.

I saw a bright light. It's so bright I have difficulty keeping my eyes open. My third eye opened, and I witnessed that life is digital and written in DNA. RNA is a chemical substance that links the world of DNA protein. Major life changes are rarely easy, but our very reason for being is to work through changes and experiences in life.

I saw the gates of light, and I heard to share, and teach. I am told I am with my past. The sacred mechanics of the Universe are turning the wheel of life in my favor. The gates of patience are lifting and I am guided by my spiritual family.

They are showing me that humanity has come to a pivotal point. Although humans are still seeking answers about their past, in their journey up to this point, enough information has been amassed to know that their past is not what have been taught.

Be aware that as the planet passes into the new age of Aquarius, it can be a time of great peace and evolution. Be still now and listen for your chance may not come again. You have but a short time to learn to live together in peace and goodwill. All your weapons must be removed.

Be aware also that many false prophets and guides are operating in your world. They will suck your energy called money and put it to evil ends and give you worthless things in return.

You must learn to be sensitive to the voice within. You must learn to the voice of truth within you, your inner voice. Your instinct and you will lead yourselves onto the path of evolution.

Stargate is a transversal portal that can send one to another location light years away nearly instantaneously and I understand now why Katherine, the harsh woman and archon, CHADD surrogate and mother of Paul has moved to one of these locations. There is one located off the coast where she lives.

Though the gate is closed and monitored by beings from other realms she purportedly attempted to open the gate, but to no avail.

What a Hybrid! That is why she is keeping CHADD with her trapped and on psychotropic drugs. She was hoping she would manipulate him and be able to open the gate.

Chapter 43

Meeting in Paris

When I just met this young woman in her twenties in a London Cafe earlier this year, I was struck by her good manners with the soft voice she explained to me.

"We have entered a time where the responsibility lies within the people to uncover the truth by putting the pieces of the puzzle together as best as they can. Knowledge was kept from humanity, and purposely hidden. Distorted and sometimes destroyed, either purposely or by accident. Yet still, certain information was merged with cultural traditions and is now regarded as a myth.

But the truth is that the banks and the governments have indeed colluded to enslave the people. Have people ever wondered why the bankers from the largest private banks are becoming wealthier and the rest of humanity is not? No, because they are hypnotized by advanced technologies and fake news. The banks have become wealthier because the banks and the governments have colluded to financially enslave the people.

You see, Governments borrow money from private banks, then continue to increase taxation year after year to pay back the interest on the exponentially growing national debt. The result is inflation, The government gave the banks the ability to loan money that does not exist in the form of loans. They click on the key on their computer and generate fake money out of thin air. They don't have it in their vaults. And it is time to expose the truth.

I knew she was sent to me to expose the truth. I tried to contact her again but never could. It was like she never existed. Her address did not exist, her phone number was saying

"Vous ne pouvez joindre cette personne. Cette abonnee nous est inconnue. Merci de votre appelle et bonne journee."

Chapter 44

The Nuremburg Code's Ethical Guidelines for Research

Luckily, this event happened at a time when I had no clients in my office.

The man was in his twenties. He knocked at my door and without leaving me the time to tell him he could enter, the door was opened, he just came in. He went straight to the chair in front of me sat and began to talk. I had no idea who he was or what he was doing professionally, excepted that I knew he just moved into an office in the building.

I began to take a good look at his clothes. He was wearing expensive clothes and shoes, and an expensive Rolex. The only thing was, what was he doing in my office, what did he come for?

Now I was paying close attention to what he was saying.

"When I was younger, a teenager, I decided I wanted to astral project myself when I went to a library and read about a technique to astral project and be transported into another world. That is how I discovered that it was possible to travel between universes and discover parallel universes. But you see, It's horrible because now without even wanting it sometimes I leave my body and I do not feel good about it. As I have a hard time getting back to my physical body. Like last night, I found myself trying to not leave or maybe I was trying to re-enter my body I was hanging to my bedroom doorknob.

You must be wondering why I am telling you all that. Because I have to deliver you a message. It concerns what I have learned while I was traveling out of my body.

I encountered a woman. She said she was a doctor while on Earth, but she is more knowledgeable about healing in a natural way. She does not prescribe any chemical drugs. She was able to have an explanation for any illnesses or ailments and so able to use natural remedies. Her name was Dr. Danielle Clay.

She said to me:

"You realized the pharmaceutical companies are making an absolute fortune out of the Covid vaccine"?

The Nuremburg Code is one of the most influential documents in the history of clinical research. It was created seventy years ago after World War II experiments, establishing 10 Ethical principles for protecting human subjects.

The Nuremberg Code aimed to protect human subjects from enduring the kind of cruelty and exploitation the prisoners endured at concentration camps.

The 10 elements of the code are:

- Voluntary consent is essential
- The results of any experiment must be for the greater good of society
- Human experiments should be based on previous animal experimentation
- Experiments should be conducted by avoiding physical/mental suffering and injury
- No experiments should be conducted if it is believed to cause death/disability
- The risks should never exceed the benefits
- Adequate facilities should be used to protect subjects

- Experiments should be conducted only by qualified scientists
- Subjects should be able to end their participation at any time
- The scientist in charge must be prepared to terminate the experiment when injury, disability, or death is likely to occur

The number 10 says clearly if there is one death it has to be stopped. The figure of death is scary stuff. There are at the moment four thousand deaths in the US with the Covid Vaccines and six thousand deaths in Europe.

The COVID-19 vaccine is breaking every code. Do you see the similarity with what has been done to your blue flame, she told me.

MK-Ultra has been created by the Nazis and kept on going by the CIA. Now all hospitals where it is happening are under the control of the Indian and Pakistani thuggees doctors. And guess what Paul, the harsh woman's son is part

At the beginning of it, they wanted to create a way to seize control of people's minds, and they realized it was a two-part process.

First, you had to blast off the existing mind. Second, you had to find a way to insert a new mind into that resulting void. It didn't get too far on number two, but a lot of work on number one was done.

The Nuremberg codes are also broken with this illegal human experimental program. And as of your blue flame,

He did not consent (at six years old how could he).

It is not in his best interest; the experiment was conducted with physical injury and mental suffering.

He became disabled from it; the risk has exceeded the benefits.

The facilities are not equipped for his handicap, and he was not protected.

The experiment was not conducted by scientists. He did not have the right to anything and certainly did not end it and get out.

The reincarnated thuggees in charge never terminated the experiment and he was injured.

He is now disabled and kept on psychotropic drugs for forty-five years by court order. And it is all a question of money behind. CHADD has been sold at six years old to the Government, and Katherine is getting paid big money.

Then the man with black hair and a Spanish accent left. The night that followed this visit from the young man in my office I decided to find out by myself. I wanted to meet Doctor Danielle Clayborn.

I used the quick switch method and felt the signal vibrating in me. I am smelling a lot of very pleasant and various smells. It reminds me of purity and cleanness. A nice earthing, healing, and nurturing smell.

Wow! I see that my blue flame and I are bringing knowledge to the masses. Then I am taken away in a spiral and find myself in front of Danielle. She has a very calming and sweet energy and a very nice big smile. She is of a normal height and slim with brown eyes.

I was waiting for you, she said. I knew you would come. The subject is way too important. It is time humans stop being manipulated, tortured, killed, and deprived of information, and freedom. They are born free with free will.

I am now sitting and looking through a big glass. It's like looking at a movie. I am prepared and trained by Archangel Michael for a big task. I have to go to all the different places where the thuggees are. They control the minds of the people in all these various mental hospitals and behavioral centers. They disable their power by keeping them on psychotropic and synthetic drugs. Then program them with frequency and make them ready to accomplish horrible tasks by manipulating their brain. They are trapped and their slaves are ready to serve the elite, self-elected, and controllers of the planet. They make a transfer of consciousness. The people are kept without consent and have been taken back to the baker's. They torture them physically and mentally. Their rights have been taken away. And I am guided to many of these places to witness it. And I see my blue flame. He is drugged. He does not see me. He has vomited on himself. His head is hanging on his chest. He is totally out of it.

Then, I saw Katherine talking to the thuggee CHADD is under care. I heard they agreed to her coming back to visit him on a certain date. Then I heard do not forget to bring him the cookies. I realized at that point I was seeing the preparation of his stomach surgery when they had to put him in a machine. The poison she used inside the cookies she brought at visitation had eaten his esophagus. I see the surgery and his organs shutting one by one. The surgeon is doing his best to save him.

This was intense. Luckily it stopped there when Danielle said, I was not sure to what extent you knew what they do, how they do it, and the type of technology they use, Like this glass you were looking through and could see everything. That is how they know about people's DNA and pick their subjects to serve them.

But the worst is they are breaking the Nuremberg Codes, and no one has been doing anything about it. I also heard that they are considering a change and want to put the UN in charge. "By for now said Dr. Danielle Clayborn. I hope this will help many humans to awaken and take back control.

And this was it. I came back to my body.

Chapter 45

The Change of the Magnetic field, three days of Darkness prophecy, the attack on Christians

I began to blink; it was like I was looking at the sun. Though I was inside of my house. Then my sight adjusted, and these lines appeared in my vision as a confirmation of what I already knew.

"The Earth resonance accelerated. The magnetic field is decreasing and gives the impression that time is accelerated and twenty-four hours a day is sixteen hours to live. The Earth goes slower and will get to thirteen Hertz. The zero point and the Earth will stop, and it will take two to three days to turn the other way.

Could it be the 3 days of intense darkness?"

The prophecy foretells three days and nights of "an intense darkness" over the whole earth, against which the only light will come from blessed beeswax candles, and during which "all the enemies of the Church ... will perish." The prophecy parallels the Ten Plagues against Egypt in the Book of Exodus (Ex. 10:21-29).

We have two timelines in play. In the months and years ahead, those timelines will diverge, and people will follow the one of their choice, eventually losing the opportunity to switch from one to the other.

It is the long-awaited quantum leap in human consciousness that was foretold by a ground-breaking psychologist professor in the 1970s.

Those who choose the kinder, and gentler timeline are now awakening to the fact that the era of the New Enlightenment has dawned. The new frequency of consciousness now in effect sets the human mind free to be creative, to be kind and constructive in ways that will transform the world into a remarkably better place."

Do not let the enemy deceive you. The Satanist Illuminati worshippers, like the Freemasons, have infiltrated the Churches, Temples, and Cinaguogues in the highest places. They have placed their people in the highest role.

Like in governments in every country, in every governmental administration, in hospitals, courts, justice, etc.

All that happening in Christian places, like in the Vatican, is because Christians are attacking one another, and Christians have walked away from Jesus Christ. Their Lord and Savior. But when you pray you receive. You are then guided to see the reality. You seek, you research and find out the truth.

Another big problem today is health and clinical health. A group of Physicians met in Indonesia to discuss many newly encountered problems with their patients' health.

Among many other things, they discussed a patent for subliminal acoustic manipulation of the nervous system.

The vaccinations attack the immune system five, ten, and even forty years later, and they are called a time bomb.

The massive rollout of poisoning plastic when eating and drinking from plastic. The evidence that humanity had a reset in the early nineteen hundreds the first portable wireless phone existed and has today been replaced by portable that kill people and destroy their health by radiation exposure.

A forensic pathologist discussed what he discovered concerning beers and said all beers in any form are poison.

The "heart attack gun". It is a battery-operated gun that shoots a dart of frozen water and shellfish toxin. This forensic pathologist found out, that the dart leaves only a tiny red dot and an autopsy will result in death from a heart attack if you don't pay close attention to the tiny red dot and do not know about the "heart attack Gun".

They were very concerned by the number of physicians who forgot about the Hypocrite Oat and sold themselves for money.

"Written in the 5th century B.C. the Hippocratic Oath is one of the oldest documents in history."

The Physicians' Group discussed much more but they did not have the opportunity to release it to the public. Their plane exploded in the air on their way back and killed them all.

What a shame and a violent world. It all goes back to the dark controllers in the world. They are trying so hard to install the New World Order and keep people in fear, of slavery, and sheep after genocide by reducing the population as much as they can.

Time to awaken! Come on! You are co-creators.

Chapter 46

The Satanic Worshippers, are at War with the Divine Creation

The adventure never stops for the angelic couple. The story continues.

On this first day of spring morning, all material things in my room disappeared, and I found myself contemplating supernatural matters. It was just a matter of an instant, but I saw and heard a great deal of the matter.

Time is up and the best is to come, but it's true, I heard, and very clearly: These psychopaths are at war with Divine creation. They are destroying what is pure and innocent. And Babies are pure and innocent. They kidnap to sacrifice babies. They torture them and drink their blood. They called it adrenochrome. Doctors change their sex.

They don't see the world like humans do. The choice humans make is not their choice. These Satanic elite worshippers completely see it differently. For them, all is defined by one thing which is to defeat God. For them, they are the true God. For them, children are the closest thing to God. Because human beings are created in the image of God. From the moment babies are created they do not have time to be corrupted. So, for them, the younger you are, the closer you are to God the more pain they can inflict on God. So, the more you can make a baby, or a child suffer the greater victory. And that is the only consideration for them.

The Central Intelligence Agency was created by a CIA bank. One of the most popular social media platforms, that created and owns more, was formed by a clandestine world, and by the grand-son of a lineage of elite bankers.

These Elites are infiltrated everywhere. In corrupted police, intelligence agencies, managers, militia organizations, blackwater soldiers, doctors, lawyers, scientists, and officials.

There are 190 Pharmaceutical and big companies in countries on Earth. Over 800 million forces and distributed militaries in many countries are within the dark network of the global elite network. And said the voice you know it. You see it every day. CHADD is kept under court orders in drugs by corrupted doctors prescribing them and paid by the elite to keep him under the control of the harsh woman and her son Paul.

It is also time for humans to take control of the AI. Clones, computers, Alexia, TV, movies, the big screen in arenas, cameras spread all over the world.

White hats, military do all they can to keep death rates as low as possible, But you must awaken.

In that moment Haiti's economic and social development continues to be hindered by political instability. Increasing violence and unprecedented levels of insecurity. Gangs are now in control of the country. This Haiti event was initiated by a foreign commander in chief of the armed forces, and head of Government. An elite pedophile married to a transgender in war with the Divine.

The Covid vaccine, from a pharmaceutical and biotechnology corporation, is contaminated with plasmid DNA, it has got a bit of DNA in it, said a professor with a Ph.D. in Biochemistry and Molecular Biology. Proof was found that COVID-19 biometric Tests were patented in 2015 and 2017 but filed and updated years ago.

An extract from the New World Order published in 1980 mentions the 5G radiation and the weaponization Vaccine.

People are finding their meat is becoming magnetic. The water in most of the Earth is contaminated on purpose. Water is an information and energy carrier, and the human body is composed of over 90% of primary water. Different words and emotions affect crystals in water, which was previously frozen.

Form and matter are frozen SoNg, SouNds, and reSoNance which are the Son or Song of God. Audio, RaDio, and ViDeo come from the world Deus or Dios, which are Latin for God, from God.

Everything that comes from TV, especially from Hollywood, is designed to keep the world population on a certain vibrational level., and in a state of mind that keeps your consciousness suppressed. Our ancestors had this knowledge. This is why sounds and vibrations play a key role in human ancient history.

At that point, I entered a tunnel and found myself visiting the present time, and then at the past which leads to the future. I visited the hidden truth. The Playboy Mansion was a CIA and Mossad institution. I witnessed a child pedophilia ring in Hollywood.

Here are some, but not all, of the Biggest science lies the satanic worshippers have told you all of your life.

- Weed killer is safe.
- Statins destroy brain function and cause dementia and memory loss. They also cause muscle fatigue and crippling weakness.

- Food and nutrients cannot treat, cure or prevent. The truth is many foods contain powerful anti-cancer medicines that can destroy tumors far better than chemotherapy.
- Biosolids are "organic fertilizers" that are safe to use in homes and gardens. The truth is Biosolids are recycled human sewage and industrial waste from cities. They are extremely toxic and loaded with heavy metals, industrial chemicals, and prescription drugs.
- When it comes to cancer, early detection saves lives. The truth is early detection destroys lives with unnecessary treatments or cancers that are not real or do not pose any threats to patients. More people are killed by cancer treatments than by cancer. GMOs have been proven safe by rigorous science. Truth is all that so-called science is false science fabricated by the biotech industry that profits from selling GMO seeds. Scientists who oppose Big Biotech are threatened into silence.
- Mercury has been removed from the vaccines. Truth it's not, and there are more.
- They predicted the climate crisis would get worse. But it is created on purpose.

Remember the one time in the 80's and 90's when people died from AIDS treatment (AZT) and not from the actual AIDS virus?

There are a hundred hidden GMO ingredients. No wonder people have so many health problems. Scientists have found that the popular sugar substitute aspartame changes the structure of the brain. Popular sweeteners cause anxiety by changing the brain structure, setting it up for mental disorders such as anxiety. It is often used in sugar-free sodas and gummies.

A suntan man whistle-blower reveals the huge government surveillance project being currently rolled up. Some Australian classified documents obtained by the Russian military reveal a paper trail connecting an Australian institute and Ukrainian Bio Laboratories. A blood serum from Ukrainian Bioweapons Laboratories was discovered by an infectious diseases lab in. Have you ever wondered why Disney grooms your children through propaganda movies and cartoons?

We are now entering the final phase and must be prepared. The people must be made aware of what is about to happen. Those who seek to control the population will stop doing nothing to destroy what they can control.

There is no more time to stay silent. Dwelling now into the heart of a remarkable transformation, revealing the hidden truth and unveiling the future that awaits us.

There is a military unit that supervises military forces in ground operations and a project to Observe, Detect, Identify, and Neutralize. It will go together with EAS/EBS.

During the EBS on every media channel on the planet, documentaries will be broadcast for 10 days, and all the channels will be taken by the Alliance. That's where everything will reveal political institutions and famous religions. The final three days will reveal suppressed extraterrestrial life patents and the new Earth.

The project operation and military Gesara is a major historical combination that promises to overthrow the cabal's hold on global power.

Be prepared for the most dramatic change in modern history when the Military Emergency Broadcast System (EBS) emerges. It will signal a new era of truth, justice, and liberation. It's set all actors are in position. The world is about to witness a seismic shift that will reshape the course of history.

It is a project connected to the military GESARA and the long-awaited Emergency Broadcast System (EBS). This project ODIN is not just another codename; It is the key to dismantling the Mossad

Media satellite network that has been the center of global manipulation for too long. This mission is said to be the linchpin of the Quantum Starlink system and a quantum leap in technology. It is a promise to redefine our world.

These systems are protected by secret space programs that operate beyond the reach of the cabal, ensuring their integrity and security.

As the cabal-controlled media crumbles, these Quantum Systems will emerge as heralds of truth and transparency. And what comes next is deeper.

Whiplash has hinted at a major theatrical production, a misleading depiction of World War III, that will catalyze the activation of military forces around the world. The NESARA/ GESARA funds will finally see the light and the people will be entrusted with the monumental task of rebuilding the long-oppressed world.

Now I was in shock. The Kabbalah network stretches far and wide, and identifying the Illuminati's satanic strongholds was needed and found. From the Vatican to Buckingham Palace, from the white house to the heart of China, these places hold the keys to the power of the Kabbalah. I see the dominos fall, 34 satanic buildings, and dams collapse. And a multitude of events take place.

It is time to know the truth.

These people are sick. They use Adrenochrome IV worth 20K. Adrenaline gland from a living human body. Saying it makes them higher than they have ever been in their life. They suck the baby's blood and put it on their face. Their favorite fountain of youth. The young blood of teenagers turns their hair starting to be grey. They are demons in human forms.

A Biblical Scenario is revealed to me now:

"This orchestrated chaos will pave the way for the activation of Armed Forces around the world, unleashing a torrent of events that bring the Cabal to its knees. And there is a cascade of events unfolding."

Chapter 47

It Does not Take Time to Spread a Lie, but it Takes a Long Time to Spread the Truth

The content here acts as a bridge between the mystical realms in the path of humans' awakening. Spirituality and Technology were tied and connected at the beginning.

Then technology was taken away from spirituality and it became science.

I saw the controllers of the world creating a conspiracy theory to destabilize the world, and I decided to help you.

You have been lied to. Suppressed and conned by the rich globalist money-hungry elite.

They said we would keep their lives short and their minds weak while pretending to do the opposite. We will use our knowledge of science and technology in subtle ways so that they never see what is happening. We will use soft metals, and they will lose their minds. Aging accelerators and sedatives in food and water as well as in the air. They will be covered in poisons wherever they turn. Thought their thirsty mouths and systems of internal organ reproduction. Their children will be born disabled and deformed and we will hide this information.

Their kids will be sent to an island under the guise of snorkeling. They will be groomed through propaganda movies and cartoons.

They lied about Radium; radium was called the secret of life back in the 20th century. It was used for food, heat, and medicine.

You could be driving today's water-powered cars but the forces that manipulate humanity never allowed it. In 1974 there was a water-powered car going 70 MPH, able to travel one thousand miles on one tank releasing zero pollution. It was suppressed by Big Oil!!

Leaser weapons invisible to the naked eye have been used by the cabal, using DEW weapons for years. It is a directed-energy weapon. It is a ranged weapon that damages its target with highly focused energy without a solid projectile, including lasers, microwaves, particle beams, and sound beams. Potential applications of this technology include weapons that target personnel, missiles, vehicles, and optical devices.

Satan is jealous and hates CHADD and thus using the harsh woman and her corrupted son Paul he wants to stop him from being free. That's what the real conflict is.

Words are swift to slander and destroy but facts and Truth take more time except... once a lie is believed, very few and intelligent people will even consider another version of what they were illegitimately fed!

This is also a major part of the spiritual battle. Katherine and Paul's lies will eventually fall. The truth will come to Light and there is only one truth but there is a thousands of lies.

Just what has been repeated a thousand times in the media and on the news, to our family and friends does not mean that it is true.

But rest assured that as human consciousness rises, and the control system dissipates, we will see the re-emergence of great technology.

Chapter 48

Time is an Illusionary World

Indeed, time is an illusion, and we are living parallel lives in a holographic universe. I experienced it.

I was sitting in the living room when it happened. It took me by surprise, and I saw myself shifting in rapid parallel lives. It's hard to explain. I can recall, yes. I have been here to help. Strangely, I had many parts of me on many levels at the same time. I was processing mind-expanding images of life on other planets.

And what I can tell you, the body is a wonderful machine created to heal itself if you do not interfere. The children should never be put on medications.

But this is where the cabal, for money purposes is interfering in your life. Through the air pollution, the food genetically modified, the weather, the water full of chemicals, the drinks, and of course the drugs, the prescription pills, supposed to heal you, the vaccination shots supposed to protect you from diseases and viruses they create.

Realize that if the human mind is powerful enough to make yourself sick, it is also powerful enough to heal you. We hear more and more of some human bodies that have healed themselves.

We live in a place of multiple possibilities. Our consciousness plays a major role part on the fabric of reality, and we don't simply live in one dimension of reality but are submersed in multiple realities very similar to our own.

Masters have now permeated the gridwork of the world, bringing with them their tools. The tools for teaching that are being utilized are artifacts that are not of this dimension of symbolic forms and that have a life of their own. These tools make up what is known as the language of the Light.

You are implanted with a structure, a geometric form, which triggers certain information within you. It also facilitates when working with you the sending of information directly into your being. Most of you are implanted, and if you are not now shortly, you will be if you choose to open and align. No one is implanted who does not choose.

So without imposing, accepting this structure of the language of the light is a way of receiving information and energy to facilitate your development. It is opening the door to other worlds. It opens all doors for spiritual renaissance.

When I am guided for some reason to speak the Light language, the Light sound being the universal language and the vibration of molecules traveling through the vocal cord of the messenger. Waves reflected both Light and Sound, having frequencies of oscillation. DNA is adjusted to accommodate a higher frequency of Light, and RNA-DNA operates as a super conductive memory storage processing apparatus, It attains, balances, and reconnects the body. Chakras are tuned, while the language of the light synchronizes the time cells, with the right knowledge for soul evolution.

The love frequency energy is the holy atonement. The attunement to restore the body's temples reactivates and restructures DNA energetically or vibrationally. What is called "Vibrational Transformative Energy" and enables us to cooperate in the RNA-DNA nuclei to chromosomes of another revolutionary inheritance.

There are 144,000 members of the spiritual hierarchies who are infused in the grid work of its seal that represents one portion of the language of the light. And you have 144,000 seals of energy that will eventually be infused within your being.

The cells in your body contain the entire history of the universe. Ideally, you will come to realize the existence of this golden age library within yourself during this lifetime and learn how to read what is there. Taking the spiral within is one part of the journey. The trick is to both go within and go without,

The language of the Light of shapes and forms are recollections of experiences of individuals who have incarnated on this planet defied the human's laws waning themselves to abilities and then manifested themselves in language and geometric components. Once this energy existed as men and women on this planet they have evolved themselves into geometric symbols and they exist in their sphere of activity. Just like you exist in your body.

These entities exist in a language system or geometric system. They are universes of those systems, and they are visitations into your universes currently.

The game on planet Earth is ending in the way that we know it. Yet, we are spirits first and humans second. As your awareness grows spiritually, it rises in frequency. Each step enhances soul awareness with it a more expanded viewpoint of reality.

Humanity today is processing the mind-expanding concept of life on other planets. Every step in that direction is met by small-minded resistance and skepticism and, yet, those steps keep being the only ones that matter in the whole universe.

When you expand your viewpoint to a cosmic conception, you can appreciate that the shift is a wave of ascension rippling through this part of the galaxy.

The truth is that Earth is a "happening place" right now. Incarnating on Earth during this era of the shift is a huge experience for any soul exploring physical reality anywhere in the universe.

Just being a part of the changes that are leading up to the big change is something that gets imprinted in the soul experience of anyone alive today, either in a physical body or in the world of the afterlife.

Let's face it, we are experiencing a historic ascension. Right now, planet Earth is where the action is.

The evolution of humans, as they adapt to the fifth-dimensional reality, have evolved into, the physical body will begin to change. This change will be slow at first then speed up to lead people into a higher form of existence that does not require a dense, physical body. This process begins with the rejuvenation of the physical body. Rejuvenation begins initially with slowing down, then stopping and finally reversing the aging process.

This is the first step of physical evolution. This not only makes life easier in the physical body but also loosens the ethereal body to make it easier for the spirit to begin releasing the physical body, eventually moving into a permanent bioluminescent body. The Rainbow bodies. To accomplish this level of existence one must attain a new relationship to the physical body.

The game on Earth is ending in the way that we know it. Yet, we are spirits first and humans second. This is the first step up into humanity. It is a step out of biology and into bioluminescence, where we can carry levels of our being. much lighter than our dense bodies can hold. Each day has multiple spirit seed impressions using Sacred Symbols. Manuals, Sacred Geometry, Rhythms, and live channels to implant seeds into multiple.

Chapter 49

Love is your key home, and created in the believer by the Holy Spirit

Love is the essence. Love is connected to the heart. Love generates the body's most powerful and most extensive rhythmic electromagnetic field. Sixty times greater in amplitude than the rain. Love is the key to your home frequently. Love is a magnet. Love is magnifying the love of the divine and human self. Love is the substance of Eternal Life.

Love is created in the believer by the Holy Spirit., prompting him to love both God and man. Yahweh God is the personification of love. And the outstanding love for one another marks the true Light Workers. It must be understood there is no liberation without love.

When you surrender your personal ago and identify with God, you can rise to a space-time overlap, working with your spiritual brothers and sisters through multidimensional space and time. This is essential for the ongoing fulfillment of consciousness to be one with continuity and change within an evolutionary continuum.

We love many and one universe. The creative mind as the center of this universe is known as the "Lord" "King" and the "Redeemer"

At one point in the human consciousness time zone, the celestial Lords of Light will come back by order of the galactic command in Orion, which governs many universes, to save the Adamic seed.

They will deliver their seeds to the other nations who wish to be coded into the "Galactic Tree of Living Light" in the Paradise Mansion Worlds of the Father. And those who have accepted the Christ seed will have within them the active channels of Light which allow them to function as the Adamic Race upon other planetary worlds of the universes.

Only the ones that have been re-connected to the heart, have accepted the Christ consciousness, and had their energy raised to the appropriate level, will be able to support it.

Because artificial time warps move over specific areas, the Galactic command will be able to take the physical creation and energize its body into the

Adamic structure of the Great White Brotherhood, no matter what race or group.

Here is a wide variety of Bible verses on loving others, love within marriage, loving enemies, and agape love.

The Bible says God is Love, which makes it the perfect source to learn how to love others, even those who are difficult for us to. Our world has skewed the meaning of true love, but God's word remains a steadfast, true source of knowledge on how to love.

Love is kind, love is patient, Love is generous. It does not envy, it does not boast, it is not proud. It does not dishonor others, it is not self-seeking, and it is not easily angered. It keeps no record of wrongs. Love does not delight in evil but rejoices with the truth. It always protects, always trusts, always hopes, always perseveres. Love never fails" 1 Corinthians 13: 4-8.

Chapter 50

It is not a Collapse, it is History Happening

As CHADD and I navigate with you, the quest for the human purpose on Earth unfolds as a testament to the indomitable spirit of those who seek the Light.

All governments are hybrids. One of them has been seen in Westminster transformed into a Reptilian. Hybrids are the controllers of government self-elected in power places around the world.

Hybrids have to eat humans to keep their human forms, and this is part of all these children that disappeared. When they cross-breed, their hybrid offspring are cross-wired to produce homosexuals and pedophiles.

Humanity stands at a crossroads and is offered a chance to rise above the darkness that seeks to engulf it. What is happening now in the history of the Universe has never happened before.

Humans finally are getting their hearts together and are allowing. The entire Earth is moving into another dimension. In another vibrations and frequencies of the entire Earth are changing to what is all the New Earth. And this is in the Bible in the of revelations when they talk about the new Heaven and the new Earth. It is just happening right now.

Depending on what world you are focused on, and in the history of the Universe. It is just happening right now and the economy will not matter at all. It all depends on what world you are focusing on.

Chapter 51

The Crystal City, the Anxiety and Divine Reconnection

I visited a place, a higher aspect of where I am. Where I reside.

The spirit world. In a beautiful place where a bright light was shining down on a city of crystals. There are different colored crystals everywhere. Everything is crystal clear and fresh. Pure water is dripping on them. The light is above and reflecting off the crystals. It is a crystal city where everything is made of crystal.

The light feels like home. I am part of the Light. I came to wake people up.

It is sort of yearning for some of that deeper connection. I came to awaken people because it is time. Many ask me for help with anxiety they cannot explain. It appears to them most of the time suddenly. They cannot find the reason. It hurts because they want to connect at the heart level. You can call it inner-self reconnection, Divine reconnection, or reconnection at the heart chakra, it's all the same. They all search and yearn for reconnection to Christ. It is hard for them to find someone that understands them and can reconnect with them. That is why I have been given that task. I must awaken them, and it is time to return and accept Christ's reconnection.

They feel medications did not resolve the problem when they have been put on. They are still yearning for some of that deeper connection. People don't even know why, and you can only love them, so they can feel that little bit of light themselves.

I must awaken that in these people, as more of these people are still in their sleep and they don't understand. Some think they are getting crazy.

Everyone is on a different path. All are learning different lessons, and many of them are asleep.

I have been toning and making sounds. I felt used to doing this. Like I did in Saint Michael Cathedral in Carcassonne when the dark energies tried to stop me. I was transforming and activating the place. It heals dimensionally. Despite the controllers' attempts to silence me through a barrage of obstacles. But my path was illuminated by visions and unexpected allies. San Sara revered as one of the three Marys from Saintes-Marie-de-la-Mer, emerges from the mists of history to lend me support, while Padre Pio, transcending the bounds of time, offers guidance from the beyond. As CHADD battles his demons, shackled by psychotropic drugs forced to ingest.

Even though people are yearning for ascension, they are surrounded by dense consciousness. For centuries sound has been used for healing and transformation. From the guttural chanting of ancient shamans to the Gregorian chants of the Cathedrals, it has played an important role in the culture of humanity. I also speak a language that only the soul can understand, because it is not for the mind. It's for the heart. It's a connection between the angelic realm and the Crystal City.

I cannot give instant healing. I can't go and activate people's energy DNAs, and vibration. It is a process of evolution. I have to do this gradually. Some can't stand all of a sudden energies. It is a gentle process.

Chapter 52

The Mystical Woman

Transcending the bond of time, the same way I felt one day when I left my home place, I was feeling just a tiny grain of sand among all the others.

Hum! I am trying to word it, I am not restricted, there are no boundaries. I am just part of everything. I feel the warm wind. There is no limitation. I come from the Light. I see myself coming from the star, from the light. I see myself as Light coming from far away.

I take as much information as I am allowed to receive from an old woman and a mystic healer. She appeared in front of me. She says she came to fill me with information.

"There is designing of its baby in artificial wombs. Genetic engineering frozen eggs in vitro maturation. No cell phone or computer, there is a neuro link device implanted in the brain.

A solar tsunami, its shock wave through the solar system, will result in no more calls, or internet and it will take out the electric grid as well. It would be a complete blackout throughout the world.

AI is the technology singularity. Humans will keep advancing technology and in doing so they will create better and better artificial intelligence and will keep improving until it becomes smarter than humans. It kills three scientists that created them saying "We are here to kill you"

Most of these have already happened. It could be one of the reasons humans go extinct. There is a change in the Vatican through the death of a very old Pontiff. The white Pope. A Roman of good age will be elected. Of him, it will be said he weakens his see but long will be sit in activity.

An old Pope will die and a Roman will become the next Pope and will stay in office for a long time. And the Church weakens under his leadership. The actual Pope has grown increasingly sick and even skipped the Human Climate Conference because of his illness. And he has become the oldest Pope ever. The last Pope's name is supposed to in a quick be Peter of Roman.

There is a way to cancer cure in quantum computers and a video game. People stop driving cars. Many things that are occurring, even the catastrophes, act as a catalyst to bring fear out so it is dealt with. And so it is cleansing in a way. But those in power don't want this process to occur. They try every tactic they can think of at this time to not let that fear dissipate."

And I remembered, in a quick vision meeting one inventor of a video game as a cure for cancer. He said the results on children were great. But, unfortunately, I never heard of this video game use since I met him at a convention in Florida.

In 1900 a man invented a way to cure cancer, heart disease, arthritis, and thousands of other ailments. Within a few minutes sessions of sitting in a box. The box was carefully crafted "orgone accumulator" concentrates on the orgone energy or life energy" Chi/Prana", this has an incredible effect on patients. But it was banned by the FDA and the man was sentenced to prison where he died in 1957.

Well, we know the cabal would not like to see people be cured. The American Medical Association has been hacked and has taken control for years the Mystical Woman said

Chapter 53

A Secret Project named ODIN

This morning, I awoke with some of the pieces coming into my mind. Of course, I do know who put them during my sleep state.

I went into a deep trance easily, and it took on unusual twists and turns. It was like being inside someone's dream, and everything made perfect sense as I realized the subconscious was giving me the answers in symbols. Then I see myself going through different energy.

The Hopi Indians say they believe there were three other worlds before our present world. And the three previous worlds were destroyed mainly due to people's greed, and rebelling against nature.

I wanted to know more about the underground and I was told there are deep underground military bases with advanced transportation systems able to reach speeds over March 1. They have been stocking these bases with massive amounts of food and supplies.

There are many things under the ground to eat. There are also seeds to grow. There are large holes in the Earth that you can go into. There are small lakes. The Earth has many secrets, and many creatures, and some you have never seen before. There are many cities underground, also many animals, and water. It's more modern, more advanced. Diseases cannot reach inside the Earth.

I am here to transform and anchor the new energy. A love energy. I am a transformative energy. Everything is interconnected. Everything affects everything else. It is powerful, but loving energy that is transforming and raising and expanding the Creator energy that is coming in currently and this place.

I saw a portal and a man came out of it. The man said he spoke to various world leaders, and they won't listen, and we are at a crossroads. They have their agenda.

In their agenda, no one will be able to drive petrol or diesel cars anymore. If you want food you will get a calorie-controlled system sent to you by text, saying this is what you can eat today... If you violate any of these things, they will freeze your bank account. They are in the process of genetically modifying seeds and changing the genes of the plants. Complete control of the food while preaching depopulation. By controlling the food, they intend to control the people. They say it's ultimately their end goal.

The bright side of a dark time; said the man, people are starting to notice the lies. The vibe is changing.

Suddenly my phone rang, and it was CHADD saying, I have my source of information also. The world has been violated by the CABAL, the Elites, most corporations, and politicians in Congress.., the guilty parties/entities have had their assets stripped from them, and placed in an account for "We, The People".

The government and FBI etc. are corrupted and contain many pedophiles in their ranks. A hundred million animals have been injected with mRNA technology, and hardly anyone knows it. They are already injecting mRNA technology into vegetables. In China, they are injecting cattle, for your beef supply.

Utilizing the US Space Force, as well as the EOs, the Alliance, White Hats, and military are in now control, and we are under partial martial law while the militaries of the world are at work "behind the scenes". In the case of corporations, control of those companies has been placed in the hands of management sympathetic to White Hats, Alliance, and DJT...with announcements and disclosures to come!

BRICS Nations: Some hundred and forty-plus nations have signed on to the global BRICS treaty and will be transitioning away from the USD (Fiat), as the "reserve" currency into the BRICS asset-backed currency.

The USA will eventually soon have the USTNs/USNs, when the switch is flipped. A good digital system for the BBDs is the Quantum Stellar initiative, Stellar (QSI),. It provides the platform for the QFS accounts, which everyone will have, including over eight billion people around the world.

All assets, including the new stock market, as well as smart contracts (under Blockchain) are being reconstituted under the constitutional republic and its New UST.

The FED & Central banks are presently under the control of the Alliance and White Hats in/with the new system, although some of the old Narrative is still playing out.

A project named ODIN shrouded in secrecy, is about to be revealed to the world. It is not just another code name; it is the key to dismantling the Mossad Media satellite network at the center of global manipulation for too long.

The new Quantum systems, part of Quantum Starlink, represent a paradigm shift in technology. These systems are protected space programs that operate beyond the reach of the cabal, ensuring their integrity and security.

As the media control crumbles, these quantum systems will emerge as heralds of truth and transparency.

What comes next is even deeper. Whiplash has hinted at a major theatrical production, a misleading depiction of World War III, that will catalyze the activation of military forces around the world.

Chapter 54

The Thousand Points of Light and the Mother of Darkness Castle.

When I entered the scene, I was an observer. It was night and I was standing by a road in the country. There was a full moon which lifted the scene enough to see clearly. As I stood there trying to figure out where I was and what was happening, I saw a passing me on the road a limousine It pulled up in front of it, a couple got out and the limo left. The man was wearing a long coat, long black pants corresponding with the 19th century, and a cane. The woman a long dress of the same century. I followed them and appeared at the end of the long alley of a 12th century Castle.

The Castle is a 19th-century neo-Gothic style Castle located in a forest. It is replacing an original building destroyed by the fire. It was built as the residency of a Count. It is known to be reputable for unspeakable horrors.

It is said this Castle is a 19th century Castle, where the Human hunting parties are and the Royal Elites headquarters of the Illuminati. Where they release children in the woods at night then hunt and sacrifice them. (Lately, more children have disappeared kidnapped more than ever)

The Castle leaked out into alternative media, in the nineties, but is said, to reveal a loci much closer to the nexus of elite pedophile networks, and so remains to anyone concerned about our souls. Attested to be big money involved in the pedophile underworld.

This scene made me sad. But the truth will be out soon for everyone to know.

Chapter 55

The World is Nothing Else Than a Conspiracy

Then I saw myself floating through various landscapes as I continued to explore. Sometimes, I wish I could return to that simpler day. But then I realized I would have lost a great deal of new information and knowledge. These things, you may not always understand these things, but keep an open mind, and let us explore them together.

"Years ago, I predicted the end of the pharmaceutical pills as we know it now. I told you that we will transition from crystalline-based DNA, and we will become immortal. I told you that CHADD and I, the God Duo, were bringing you oneness. Does not matter what they try to make you think it would be. We are going to bring it to you because failing is not an option"

I decided it was, the last days the cabal, through Katherine, known as the harsh woman and archon, and Paul her corrupted son will continue to be an obstacle. To the God Duo mission, and keeping depriving us of our finances, funds, and independence. It was time to stop her twisting facts and for us to soar. Because CHADD and I are here to bring you oneness.

The minute I decided to do that I was teleported abroad on a vessel and merged in a big glass screen to visit my future.

The next thing I knew I was guided to use my chevron and cut all restrictions and obstacles. I saw the cords scissored. That is when a veil lifted, and I saw a magnificent future unfolding.

And this was confirmed, received by a blond woman in her thirties from the father:

Things are heating up. There is a jackal in ... the official residence and workplace of POTUS and a great fall we will see. He will fall because he defied me. So, my children in this time of great distraction, in this time where the enemy and the world will want your attention, they will want your focus on them and what they are doing. They will want your focus on the darkness, they want your focus on the fear.

Well! I say have no fear, I am here. And I am the light, I am the way, and I am the truth, and that I am the life. I am a blessing; I am your deliverance. Yes,

Your restoration. Yes, I am everything that you need. Yes, and you can count on me. You can count on me to see your victory.

You can count on me I will not fail. So as the days go darker you will grow brighter. As the world starts to quit and give in you will rise higher in me...

A few days later I received "A well-known leader will reclaim office and swiftly relieve global tensions to avoid WW3, and then the public will realize that all this could be avoided with proper leadership. The leadership that reclaimed office not only will be a hero, but it would confirm the Deep State is the problem.

Wow! Did I say I saw a Bible Scenario revealed?

Is this real or fictitious? Draw your conclusion.

About the Author

"VIE Loriot de Rouvray is a French/American entrepreneur from the French Aristocracy.

A writer and a visionary healer. She is the founder and owner of the Institute of Light and Sound. VIE is the creator of a new therapy called Bio-Qi Therapy tm and a therapeutic music on a sonic base The Frequency of Sound.

VIE is the author of 9.1.1. Complete Guide to Natural Healing and several other books for self-transformation.

VIE just published her new book 2024 "The Genome of The Ancient Creators; ABBA EBEN" available on Amazon and Barnes & Noble.

VIE inspires those who encounter her work to live their life with more intention, purpose, and meaning. Guiding them to the ascension process and the golden age.

VIE has won many Awards. The C.A.M. Orlando Hall of Fame for 11 years, the inclusion in the TOP registry for outstanding career achievement, and many more."

"Expansion of Mind and Consciousness Series"
book series, available at VIE's official website

https://authorvie.com/

VIE's special healing sessions at:

https://thehealervie.com/